The Children Is Crying

The Children Is Crying

Congregationalism Among Black People

by
A. Knighton Stanley

The Pilgrim Press
New York/Philadelphia

Library of Congress Cataloging in Publication Data

Stanley, Alfred Knighton, 1937–
    The children is crying.

    Bibliography: p. 163
    Includes index.
    1. Afro-American Congregationalists—Southern
States.   2. American Missionary Association—History.
3. Missions to Afro-Americans—Southern States.
I. Title.
BX7147.A35S7   285′.875   78-26544
ISBN 0-8298-0347-5

The Pilgrim Press, 287 Park Avenue South, New York, New York 10010

Contents

Illustrations appear between pages 104 and 105.

Preface

This study consists of a socio-historical treatment of the American Missionary Association and renders an interpretation of the missionary movement of the Congregational churches in America, which established churches among and ministered to Black people in the southern part of the United States between the years 1861 and 1926. Although the Congregational churches united with the Christian Church in 1931 to form the Congregational Christian Churches, and although the Congregational Christian Churches merged with the Evangelical and Reformed Church in 1957 to form the United Church of Christ, no mention is made of the work among Blacks of other denominations of the union. To study the missionary endeavor among Blacks of these other parties of the union would be a different undertaking.

At present there are only a few more than one hundred of the original Congregational churches among Black people in the South. They are scattered from Beaufort, North Carolina in the Southeast, to Houston, Texas in the Southwest. Together these churches claim a membership of fewer than seven thousand persons. Until 1966 all these churches were a part of one totally Black judicatory, the Convention of the South. In 1966 these churches were integrated into new conferences determined by geographical rather than racial factors. These judicatories of the United Church of Christ are the Southern Conference, the Southeast Conference, the Central Southwest Conference, and the Indiana-Kentucky Conference.

Despite the relative insignificance of this group of churches when measured against the statistics of the predominately Black denominations, such as the National Baptist Convention and the African Methodist Episcopal Church Zion, a study of these churches commended itself as a matter of necessary and fruitful research. Few extensive studies of the historical Black church have emerged from theological circles since the Mays and Nicholson study of 1933. One could, of course, refer to Carter Woodson's classic study, *The History of the Negro Church* (1921), or to E. Franklin Frazier's study entitled *The Negro*

Church in America (1964). One is reminded, however, that Woodson wrote as a historian and Frazier wrote as a sociologist. Neither claimed theology as a discipline or ministry as a profession. It is also important to indicate that even at a time when many are interested in the construction of a Black theology, this effort is limited by the absence of a rigorous historical perspective out of which Black theology purports to have its rise.[1]

If the history of the Black church in America is a generally neglected area of study, the history of the Black churches of predominately white denominations is especially neglected. Black churches of predominately white denominations have been marginal institutions in the Black communities of the South and have seldom generated movements of spiritual awakening among Black people themselves. At the same time, we could study the missionary efforts among Blacks of all these predominately white churches. In so doing we could expect to find a common pattern in the approach to ministry of these denominations, as well as a common pattern of relationship that existed between the missionaries of these churches and the Black people. By the same token, we would also expect to find a common style of religious life in terms of worship, moral ideal, cultural habits, and so on among the Blacks whom these various white denominations served. Indeed, in their ministry among Blacks the churches of the predominately white denominations have been victims of a common history of difficulty, misunderstanding of their goals, and misjudgments in the performance of their "appointed tasks."

The study of the common history of these denominations would be a worthy but difficult undertaking since primary research is lacking. It may be noted that Mays and Nicholson, and others, dealt primarily with the emergence of patterns of Negro church life generated within the dynamics of an all-Black framework. It is my conviction, therefore, that the Congregational churches, within the limits defined (1861-1926), lend themselves well to a prototypal study because they represent a predominately white middle-class communion that has made a significant witness on the Black frontier of the South. I also believe that a study of this nature, which historically locates and analyzes the radical failure of one established middle-class denomination to make significant gains in southern Black communities, might be of worth and interest to all the American churches. Such a study should be of special interest to major Protestant denominations as they attempt to move beyond the established racial patterns, traditions, and institutions of a misconceived past in order to develop significant contemporary ministries in Black churches and Black communities in America.

We shall not attempt merely to chronicle facts with regard to the American Missionary Association as it attempted to establish and maintain Black Congregational churches in the South. Much of the material used for basic research in this study was written by the Congregational missionaries and ministers themselves. These were largely inspired people. The record they left behind is indeed a "holy history" that acknowledges the sovereignty of God and the lordship of Jesus Christ. They were not particularly concerned with recording the church's moments of success, which some later historians could measure and over which later generations could marvel and brood. They were led by a far larger purpose and vision, which lifted their mission above the realm of history and beyond the dimension of time. This study intends to take adequate account of the mood and context of this original endeavor of the American Missionary Association.

Initially one is tempted to play the role of lay sociologist and develop a theory that would explain the nature of Congregationalism among Black people in the South, past and present. There are, in fact, several theories that commend themselves for the task. If, however, the material with which we are here concerned is to be handled with integrity, it cannot be forced under the surveillance of an exclusively sociological analysis. To paraphrase H. Richard Niebuhr, although the sociological approach can explain why Congregationalism ventured south to establish churches among Afro-Americans, it would not explain the force of the "spirit" of the venture itself. While the primarily sociological approach would seem relevant to an analysis of the Black institutional or established Congregational churches, it would be irrelevant to an understanding of the dynamic church movement that produced these churches. While it could account for the differences in the Black and white Congregational churches in America, it could not explain the basic unity that these churches possess despite the diversities of their socio-psychological, racial, and "religious" histories. It could explain the "religion" of the white middle-class churches, which is dependent on race and culture, yet it left unexplained the "spirit of Congregationalism" and, indeed, the Christian *ecclesia militans*, which is free rather than bound, and aggressive rather than passive, and which transforms culture and transcends color rather than being diminished or divided by them.[2] Because of these circumstances a primarily sociological approach to this study would be inadequate.

Without denying the proper impact of sociology and history, I intend to attempt, with greater emphasis than heretofore achieved, to disclose those inner forces within the Congregational churches themselves by which they were moved to the post-Civil War Black South and by which they were propelled to each new frontier. Perhaps, too, it would not be inappropriate to call this indefinable catalyst the "spirit" of Congregationalism. We shall, therefore, offer instances from the history of Congregationalism among Blacks in the South between 1861 and 1926 that illustrate and test the fact of this inner dynamic. It is hoped that from a rigorous detailing of such instances there shall emerge suggested patterns for ministry that may be appropriated for effective mission in the churches today.

I am deeply grateful to all who have given assistance and support in this research. I am especially indebted to Dr. Leon Wright, whose friendship and spirit have had a profound influence upon my life and whose personal and scholarly interest in the history of Congregationalism among Blacks in the South permitted him to give fruitful guidance in this undertaking. I am indebted to the good people of Peoples Congregational United Church of Christ who, in granting sabbatical leave, provided time for this study. To Helen Armistead, who not only typed this material but also kept me on schedule, I owe particular gratitude. I am indebted to Dr. Wesley A. Hotchkiss, General Secretary of the American Missionary Association, who has been of great help to me throughout my educational and professional career. To my parents, Kathryn and J. Taylor Stanley, whose long years of devotion to the church and the Congregational Way have urged me on in commitment to ministry; and to my wife, Beatrice, and my son, Nathaniel, and my daughter, Kathryn, through whose beautiful spirits I especially hear the "children's cry," I am eternally indebted.

Chapter 1
"The Pregnant Source of a New Aggression"

In his monumental study *The Kingdom of God in America,* the late H. Richard Niebuhr observes that "the same institutionalism which represents the death of an old movement can be, as history amply illustrates, the pregnant source of a new aggression."[1]

The church and its ministry are constantly being called into action and new aggressiveness by the problems and needs that emerge from human communities and the necessity to move in on the challenges of new frontiers. No matter where or at what point in time the church has been sensitized to the human condition, it has responded or failed to respond, out of its awareness of its vocation, its sense of purpose, as a community gathered for action in history under the sovereignty of God and the lordship of Jesus Christ. On new frontiers the church has stood as prophet or priest, servant or master, movement or institution. It has both borne the cross and worn the crown. Historically, the church not only gathers for action in response to the human condition but also has the ultimacy of its mission always determined by the nature, quality, and ultimacy of the image that the church has of itself.

Since the concern here is to study the Congregational churches at work and in mission among newly freed Black people in the American South, it is necessary from the outset to pinpoint and interpret the circumstances, dynamics, and compulsions by which a denomination of the established middle class is led in ministry to human suffering and need.

Again H. Richard Niebuhr's insights are helpful. He writes in *The Social Sources of Denominationalism:* "Upon the whole the acquisition of a bourgeois type of religious faith is not an heroic achievement, accomplished by dramatic revolt from prevailing conceptions, but rather the product of a slow process of accommodation to the developing interests and experiences of a rising economic group."[2] It would seem, therefore, that the very nature of the church of the established middle-class or bourgeois society is that of an institution of social or economic expediency and fraternity, rather than a dynamic, revolutionary cause and movement created by social disquietude and religious awakening. The image that an institution has of itself is an outgrowth of its involvement in, reflection upon, and response to the historical situation and community from which it emerges. This institutionalized self-image—held consciously or unconsciously—is the energizing core, the vital form, around which the life and mission of a movement revolve and from which the movement receives strength and direction. This being the case, it would appear inevitable that the church of the middle class, grounded in the first instance in narrow self-interest rather than dynamic, revolutionary principles, is doomed to failure as a Christian institution. Failure is implied in the "bourgeois type of religious faith" because it does not participate significantly in an ethos seething with movement and revolution, an outgrowth of human need to which the Christian church, in word and work, has been historically a vital and creative response.

Such a conclusion, however, does not inevitably remain final in the face of particular religious movements and denominational histories. Our knowledge of the work of the Congregational churches among Blacks in the South will not allow us to draw this conclusion. The impact that the ideologies and constituency of the "bourgeois type of religious faith" have made upon the national and world communities would render any such conclusion invalid. There are numerous instances in which movements have been revolutionary forces in the shaping of society at large. However middle class or bourgeois a Christian institution seems to become, however static it appears to be, history bears witness that on occasion such a church can rise to the challenge of society and give evidence that deep within its energizing core there is life, revolutionary vision, and power.

How can we account for this power within the heart of bourgeois Christendom that has, from time to time, been so significantly evident in history? Perhaps the answer to this question lies in the origin of the middle-class churches themselves. Niebuhr has suggested: "There have been periods in religious history when the interests of the bourgeoisie have asserted themselves so powerfully as to assist materially in the founding of new churches in revolt against those organizations of Christianity which ignored their desires and needs."[3]

It is interesting, on the other hand, to note the fervor with which Ernst Troeltsch affirms what he believes to be the fact of a more consistent vitality on the part of the churches of the lower strata. Troeltsch believes that

> the really creative church-forming, religious movements are the work of the lower strata. Here only can one find that union of unimpaired imagination, simplicity of emotional life, unreflective character of thought, spontaneity of energy and vehement force of need, out of which an unconditioned faith in a divine revelation, the naïveté of complete surrender and the intransigence of certitude can rise. Need upon the one hand and the absence of an all-relativizing culture on the other hand are at home only in these strata. All great community-building revelations have come forth again and again out of such circles and the significance and power for further development in such religious movements have always been dependent upon the force of the original impetus given in such naïve revelations as well as on the energy of the conviction which made this impetus absolute and divine.[4]

Of course, Troeltsch is here referring particularly to the vitality of the "church-forming" movement of the lower class. If fully pressed, however, the logic of his assertion points to the fact that there is also a recurring dynamic within middle-class churches and, further, that this dynamic results from the original "community-building revelations" that, in the first instance, brought the middle-class churches into life. It must be said that appeal to tradition in the ordinary sense is not intended here. The response given by these institutions, when they are challenged by the realities of new situations and communities, is also "dependent upon the force of the original impetus given in [church-forming revelations] as well as on the energy of the conviction which made this impetus absolute and divine."[5] Unlike Troeltsch, we believe history amply illustrates that the kind of response he describes is potentially common to churches of all social strata. This being so, it is our further conviction that the signs of life and movement which periodically occur as word and work within the middle-class churches (often too hastily characterized as "lethargic") can in fact be explained in terms of what Troeltsch identifies as the "original impetus" by which they were given life.

Our reliance upon a broadening of Troeltsch's insights does not end here, for Troeltsch's concern goes beyond mere sociological analysis. He adds another dimension to this thought. Troeltsch is able to perceive that the "revolutionary spasms" which frequently recur in the "bourgeois type of religious faith" are not simply dependent upon the "force of the original impetus" given in "community-building" and "church-forming" revelations. He also perceives that these "revolutionary spasms" are dependent upon the "energy which made this impetus absolute and divine" as well. The religious movement is brought into being in response to a challenge, in answer to a "call." At the same time, the strength, quality, direction, and life span of any given religious movement is in large degree directly related to the strength, quality, direction, and life span of the conviction and faith of the adherents of the movement. In other words, these characteristics of the movement are directly related to the strength of the conviction and faith that the adherents themselves possess as to the challenge that summons the movement into being. If the worth-whileness and urgency of the challenge are indeed great enough, the conviction which is placed in the movement (and from which the movement proceeds) elicits an almost unqualified sanction. Thus, there is imparted to the movement an ultimacy that transcends time itself. Herein is that sense of calling whereby a people acquire a feeling of solidarity, of peoplehood, and whereby a religious movement is endowed with its vital core. Herein a people committed to a movement find that source of strength a sense of infinite purpose which characterizes a community of persons gathered for action in history at the bidding of God. It is the genius of this kind of coming together of people and holy conviction that explains the origin and character of viable religious movements. It also explains the dialectic process that gives rise to ever-new movements within the old.[6] It accounts for the "seasonal revolutionary spasms" that recur in the ranks of the "bourgeois type of religious faith." It locates the source of that deep sense of vocation and ultimacy which adherents of these movements bear within them. It explains the symptoms of new life and spirit that appear time and again in the old institutional forms of the middle-class churches.

Having laid this framework, which can be used to interpret the missionary expansion and evangelical zeal of most middle-class denominations, and having acknowledged our reliance upon the ideas of both Niebuhr and Troeltsch, we can now focus on our greatest concern, the ministry and mission of a specific denomination on a given frontier at a peculiar moment in time. The denomination was Congregationalism. The frontier was the Black South in America before, during, and after the Civil War. The time was 1862. The nation had come to realize that the Civil War was going to be far more tragic, prolonged, and costly than anyone had anticipated. Against this background of war and human misery, the American Missionary Association, later to become an official agency for ministry and mission of the Congregational churches, assembled in October for its sixteenth annual meeting at Oberlin, Ohio. The resolutions of that meeting stand out like righteous silhouettes against the lurid backdrop of carnage and despair. Here the church and its ministry stood and spoke:

Therefore be it resolved . . . that we rejoice that God in His providence had begun to burst open the gates of the Bastille in which four millions of our brethren have so long lain bound; that several thousands have already emerged to life and liberty, and other thousands and millions are already coming; and among these thousands and millions a door is open for missionary labor at once so wide and so hopeful of choicest fruits; that this Association feels pressed for many reasons to enter and occupy this field with their utmost ability—the emancipated being eminently ripe for the Gospel, eager for a knowledge of the Bible and for ability to read it, and the social and moral elevation being beyond measure valuable as a testimony against slavery, and against the fallacies and falsehoods alleged in its justification. The Association also regards this missionary work as due to the spirit of a pure Christianity, as adapted eminently to honor the Gospel and its Author, and as one which peculiarly belongs to the American people, being one of the works meet for repentance of their long and guilty oppression of the colored race.[7]

Indeed, the time was 1862. The ethos was that of a nation involved in the most painful and disruptive kind of war—civil war. The institution called to respond to this situation was the American Missionary Association, the Congregational "bourgeois type of religious faith." The new frontier upon which this institution stood and into which it moved was the Black South in the slow and painful process of emancipation and freedom. In a sense this institution saw as its frontier challenge a race of people —a race at its doors to be lifted from the lowest degradation to the levels of Christian civilization; a race plastic, quick to apprehend, prepared of God to receive the gift that the American Missionary Association alone could convey to it; a race whose Christian development would be its own, as its destiny would also be its own; a race whose evangelization in America would be the evangelization of Africa and a grand march toward the conversion of the whole world. The "church-forming revelation" which this movement had of itself was that of "the spirit of a pure Christianity, as adapted eminently to honor the Gospel and its Author, and as one which peculiarly belong[ed] to the American people being one of the works meet for repentance of their long and guilty oppression of the colored race."[8] The impetus given in this church-forming revelation was that of a new spirit of Christianity and Congregationalism stirring among the old forms.[9] The vocation of the movement was the propagation of the gospel and the social, moral, and intellectual elevation of the southern Negro people. The conviction that made this calling absolute and divine was the firm belief and "rejoicing" that among the millions of Black people in America, God had begun to break down the gates of the bastille of slavery and to open a door for the word, work, and ministry of the church—at once so wide and so hopeful that the association felt pressed to enter this new frontier and occupy it with its utmost ability. The association saw itself as a missionary society—indeed, as the church—which conserved in dynamic form the Congregational Way and the gospel of the kingdom of God.

Chapter 2

"An Old Spirit in New Form"

> The lines of recognition which bind the Congregational
> churches into a communion in any generation reach
> back across the boundaries of the generations from to-
> day through all the yesterdays to the very beginnings of
> the Church.
>
> —Douglas Horton
> *Congregationalism: A Study in Church Polity*

> All churches have an imperative responsibility better to
> prepare themselves for the increasingly difficult task of
> world redemption. Upon our churches rests an addi-
> tional obligation because of our heritage.
>
> —Frederick L. Flagley
> *The Gospel, the Church and
> Society: Congregationalism Today*

If we are to assume that the dynamic patterns of religious
movements and institutions—evidenced in life-styles, symbols,
myths, and so on—have historical continuity, then a survey of
these dynamic patterns as they recur in the life of such movements is essential to understanding what these movements are
about. As we attempt to understand the spirit of Congregationalism, as it moved into the Black South, it is therefore necessary to
identify the principles and ideals that initially gave rise to the
Congregational church in America and that endowed it with the
conviction that led it to respond to the challenge of the Negro
frontier before, during, and after the Civil War. Perhaps, too, it is
significant to show how the failure or success of the denomination on that frontier may be attributed to this spirit.

It is in many ways unfortunate that we cannot delve deeply into

7

all the historical patterns of church formation which represent uniquely the spirit of Congregationalism, some of which patterns eventually rendered it unfit for effective ministry in the Black South. We can indicate only briefly a limited number of these directions that contribute directly to our immediate purpose. Thus, a brief look at the biblical idea of the church is in order, for indeed, as Douglas Horton reminds us, "Congregationalism may be said to have been a gene in the body of the Church of Jesus Christ from the beginning."[1] By and large, to be sure, all churches claim this heritage. If, however, we are to come to an understanding of the image Congregationalism had of itself as a part of the Body of Christ as it moved into the new southern frontier, we must have some knowledge of the biblical idea of the church.

The Spirit of Congregationalism and the Biblical Idea of the Church

Karl Barth, in his *Dogmatics in Outline*, suggests that it would have been "great gain, could Luther's urgent desire have been carried out and the word 'congregation' had taken the place of the word 'church.' Of course we may find in the word 'church' what is good and true, since church means *Kyriake Oikia,* the Lord's House; or derived from *circa,* a circularly enclosed space. Both explanations are possible but *ekklesia* certainly means congregation, *a coming together*, arising out of the summons to the National Assembly which meets at the call of the messenger or else at the sound of the herald's trumpet."[2]

The Old Testament employs the Hebrew words *edhah* and *qahal*[3] to denote "congregation." *Edhah*, the older of the two words, comes from the root meaning "to appoint" and is therefore "a company assembled by appointment." *Qahal* is derived from the root meaning "to call" and originally meant, in secular usage, the assembling of men of military age for war. In its religious context it denoted that the nation Israel was brought into being by the word of Yahweh as partaker of the divine covenant and promise.[4]

The Gospel of Matthew uses the Greek word *ecclesia* rather than *kuriakon*. Just as *edhah* and *qahal, ecclesia* means a "calling out" or a commissioned assembly and is especially applicable to a religious congregation. It is surprising that the word *ecclesia* does not appear at other points in the Gospels. Nonetheless, in Matthew it occurs three times: once in Matthew 16:18 and twice in Matthew 18:17. If these are authentic sayings of Jesus, it is likely that Jesus used not the Greek, *ecclesia*, but rather the Aramaic, *kenushta*. *Kenushta*, though primarily a designation for a local Jewish congregation, may also designate the "messianic remnant" which Jesus came to call out of the Old Covenant and to reconstitute as the new eschatological community that will enter the kingdom of God in the age to come.

Ecclesia is used more frequently in the Acts of the Apostles than in the Gospels.[5] The word first designated the Christian community that gathered at Jerusalem at the preaching of the apostles and that consisted of those who, with the apostles, believed Jesus was the Messiah and were baptized and received remission of their sins and the gift of the Holy Spirit.[6] They believed, in opposition to the Jews, that theirs was the true apostolic community, an *ecclesia*, rather than a synagogue, and that they were called to be the heirs of God's full promise made real to them in Christ Jesus.

As the term *ecclesia* became prevalent and spread out of Jerusalem it assumed two meanings: a local congregational or Christian community (singular) and a composite of local congregations (plural).[7]

Paul uses the Acts designation of the Christian community in the plural and singular forms too.[8] But he adds a more restricted connotation of *ecclesia* as a local community assembled for worship[9] (a liturgical assembly) as the embodiment of the whole people of God.[10] Second, after discussing the theme of the Christian community as the Body of the Christ in 1 Corinthians 12:27, in 12:28 Paul speaks of the universal or invisible church as susceptible to local embodiment. He does not, however, speak of the Christian church or congregation as being one beside other churches, be they Jewish or pagan. The Christian *ecclesia* is an assembly of those called out by God in Christ.[11] The church (or rather congregation or *ecclesia*) for Paul (as is true in the Old and New Testaments) is not a building (*kuriakon*) or an established institution but an eschatological community called into being by the will and word of God in response to a cause, the human situation. Like the writer of Acts, Paul further illumines the idea that this "called out" community originates in God's redemptive act in Christ Jesus. The Christian *ecclesia* lives in unity with God's Messiah and participates in his life, death, and resurrection through the indwelling of God's Spirit.[12] In this sense, the church as his Body shares in the total life of Christ. It participates in the most full expression of God.

Claude Welch in his book *The Reality of the Church* gives a very adequate treatment of the notion of sharing or participating in the life and Body of Christ.[13] Basically, he defines participation as having one's being fundamentally in the being of another. It is no doubt in this sense of participation that Paul speaks of the church as one body, and it is in this sense that the familiar Pauline expressions "in" and "with" Christ are used. Paul affirms that Christians participate in the Body of Christ. They are *in* and *with* him. But this is no one-way process. Christ is likewise in and with them.[14] He participates in the life of sinful humanity. He draws humankind to himself by the fullness of his self-giving. Christ comes into the midst of humanity and makes the human situation his own. He sits where humankind sits. He participates in the life of fallen, estranged personhood. The church as a part of his living Body is an expression of Christ's real presence and work in the transformation of culture and his ministry to the human situation on ever-new frontiers.

Congregationalism as an institutional expression of the Body of Christ is historically and transcendentally linked with the idea and force that is the Christian *ecclesia*. From this idea and force emerges that sense of vocation, of having been "called out" or appointed for a particular task. The dimensions of the call are both horizontal and vertical. From this thrust that is the Christian *ecclesia*, Congregationalism acquires its image of itself and its authenticity as a part of the person and work of Jesus Christ. It is from the force of the original impetus in the Christian *ecclesia* that Congregationalism is endowed with its vital force, its entelechy, its sense and strength of infinite purpose as a community of individuals commissioned for action in history by a God who is supremely expressed in the ministry that is Jesus the Christ. It is in the light of this idea of the church that Congregationalism faces the challenge of the human situation. In this dynamic sense, Congregationalism claims historical continuity with the early Christian church, from which it receives the spirit of vocation, servanthood, and participation in the Body of Christ.

The Spirit of Congregationalism and the Age of Reform

It is also true that Congregationalism is historically linked with the recurring forces of reformation within Christianity. We shall not discuss its linkage with the Protestant Reformation initiated in the sixteenth century by Martin Luther and others, although our estimate of the impact of this movement in Congregational churches is high. The Congregational churches, on the other hand, arose out of the Reformation in England. Since the relationship between these two movements is commonly known, we shall only suggest that the concepts "justification by faith" and "the priesthood or ministry of all believers," which were prominent in the mind of Luther, were writ large upon the minds of the early Congregationalists and reformers in England as well.

Both American Congregationalism and English Congregationalism developed from a coalition of English Separatists and English Puritans. The Puritans and the Separatists both opposed the tenets of the Church of England, which again severed its connection from the Roman Church in 1558 when Elizabeth came to the throne. The conservative factor in the Church of England opposed changes in the established practices of the church. This faction was led by "most of the clergy who were accustomed to Roman Catholic customs and the . . . Queen and her advisers, who wished to avoid religious turmoil in the Kingdom and [who] also saw the power of the Crown safest under a subservient Episcopal hierarchy and with a prescribed uniformity."[15]

Now that the Roman connection had been broken, however, many Protestants wished more radical reform. They wanted to "purify" the church of "many of its forms and symbols, which they believed departures from the teaching of the New Testament; to purify also its priesthood and establish an educated spiritually minded, and zealous ministry."[16] In derision, these reformers were called Puritans. The name became a part of history.

11

Although they had no desire to separate from the church, as they failed to accomplish their reforms they came to question the whole political structure of the church. They especially questioned the authority of the bishop.

> During the five years of Elizabeth, the twenty-two years of James I, and the first fifteen years of Charles I, while [the Puritans] increased in numbers, the intolerance of them by the government increased also. . . . Some 20,000 of them emigrated to America in the years 1629-1640 to escape the repressive rule of Charles I and Archbishop Laud.[17]

Frederick L. Flagley indicates that

> there were among the Puritans some who inclined to a Congregational rather than a Presbyterian conception of the church, and hoped that the Church of England might lead in that direction. They thought of a church as a company of the regenerate rather than a whole community of saints and sinners; but they reasoned that the existing church certainly comprised such a nucleus among its members and the rest did not count. One could work for removal of the corruptions of the Church and remain in communion with its sound core. The clergy could submit to Episcopal ordination, but each local congregation should have the right to choose, or to accept or reject its own minister. . . .
>
> But there came on the scene from time to time, beginning in the reign of Elizabeth, little groups of Separatists, such as the "Brownists" and later the "Pilgrims." They opposed the dominant church primarily on the grounds of (1) qualification of church membership and (2) church polity. To them it was a fundamental principle that membership be restricted to the regenerate who had had a personal experience of divine grace. They rejected vehemently the theory that all subjects of the civil state were *ipso facto* members of an inclusive church. In polity, Christ being the only head of the Church, its organization was governed by the priesthood of all believers.[18]

Between 1620 and 1640 a few hundred Separatists and nearly

20,000 Puritans settled in America. The Pilgrims, the Separatist group, settled at Plymouth and were perhaps the earliest to arrive. The Puritans, or non-Separatist Congregationalists, settled in the Massachusetts Bay area and were the most influential of the two forces in American Congregationalism. During the first winter in Salem, many of the newly arrived Puritans became ill. Samuel Fuller, a physician and a deacon in the Separatist church at Plymouth, was summoned to care for them. This may have been the first contact between the two settlements. Shortly thereafter, Governor John Endecott of Salem wrote Governor William Bradford of Plymouth, "God's people are marked with one and yet the same mark." The two communities had made their initial contact, which was to eventually become a union of lasting historic moment.

With this brief and all too fragmentary survey of Congregationalism and its Puritan and Separatist wings, we can now draw out the broad implications that each of these parties—in terms of the image they had of themselves as church—had for later Congregationalism in America. On the basis of the perspective of our study, this will be done with respect to the nature of the Congregational churches' response to the demands of the frontier situation created by the emancipation of American Blacks.

First, we shall consider the Puritan or non-Separatist influence. By and large, the Puritans of the Massachusetts Bay area conceived their task as the transformation of the Church of England and, indeed, the transformation of the whole world. They "believed that they were creating a church and a commonwealth purely reformed according to the Word of God which would be a decisive example to old England and the world of what a community living in covenant relation with God should be."[19] They believed that they were a city set upon a hill, whose light would shine over the whole earth. It was their belief that since the existing church comprised a nucleus of the regenerate among its members, their task was not to break away from the established church or to organize a competing denomination. Rather, their task was to remove the corruptions within the church while remaining in essential communion with the nucleus of those already in it. It was for this reason that a strong denominational consciousness in the sense of a competing sectarianism and set of beliefs was not characteristic of early Congregationalism. As Douglas Horton points out, "It is basic to Congregationalism not to unchurch Christians who are not Congregationalists."[20] In light of this, Puritan Congregationalism believed itself to be a transformer rather than a competing force in relation to the established church.

It is almost imperative for us to keep in mind, however, that "transformation" of an established church, rather than "division" or "separation" from it, is the inherent strength of Puritan Congregationalism. On the other hand, the very lack of a competitive sectarian spirit may well be the weakness of a church as it approaches a new frontier or attempts to establish a "successful" institutional church. From this Puritan heritage there emerges in American Congregationalism a peculiar, almost paradoxical, blend. The Congregational churches have been a highly influential force in the shaping of American culture, society, and the "American ideal." Indeed, Congregationalism has been a self-giving, transforming power in national life. But because of its historic nonaggressive character—its failure to compete in the mere proliferation of churches—it has not fully reaped the fruits, in terms of communicants, of its efforts to transform.

The Spirit of Congregationalism and the Separatist Doctrine of Regeneration

The Pilgrims, or Separatist Congregationalists, were fewer in number and a less influential force in the development of American Congregationalism. Nonetheless, the impression they made has been great and lasting. The most vehement protest the Separatists waged against the established church was their rejection of "the theory that all subjects of the civil state were *ipso facto* members of an inclusive church."[21] It was the Separatists' fundamental, determining principle "that church membership be restricted to the regenerate who had had a personal experience of divine grace."[22] It was around this idea and protest that the Separatist group sprang into life. The church for them comprised the community of the visibly redeemed, and to this extent the church was not inclusive. The historical exigencies of sixteenth- and seventeenth-century England seemed to justify this protest.

It is possible, however, that in later moments of the history of the church this exclusive—or, better, elective—tendency loses touch with its original historical and theological intent, so that only the spirit of exclusiveness—based on social and economic class— remains. As Hugh Vernon White points out, this demand for a visible sign of regeneration made each person a sort of inquisitor into the inner life of others. Few people "can be accorded this right without misusing it."[23]

The insistence that church membership be based upon the indi- vidual experience of God's grace rather than mere consent to theoretical formulations of religious beliefs had further implica- tions for Congregationalism in America. Both the Puritan church at Salem and the Separatist church at Plymouth were established on the basis of a covenant not a creed. "Whether one could be called a Christian, and so admitted to full membership in the church, depended not upon . . . Baptism as a child nor . . . acceptance of a creed, but upon the reality of the working of God within [one's] soul making [one a new person] in Christ and giving [one] the assurance of salvation."[24] This absence of creedal for- mulations and the lack of the embodiment of the idea of the church in symbols and practices laid the basis for the "liberal- izing intellectualism" characteristic of the Congregational spirit.

> Congregationalists have had their creedal controversies,
> and their history reveals sufficient dogmatism in matters
> of religious belief; but the refusal on principle to recog-
> nize any formulation of faith as binding and definite has
> created a freedom of thought which has enabled Congre-
> gationalism to absorb with a minimum of difficulty new
> ideas and interpretations of Christian doctrine.[25]

This "liberalizing" tendency—resulting from a covenantal rather than a creedal, doctrinal, liturgical, or hierarchical understanding of the church—certainly has bearing upon the degree of flexibility of the Congregationalists' response to a new frontier. Certainly, flexibility and dialogue among a new people in a new situation is advantageous, even imperative. But, as will be seen later, this very lack of identifiable practices, symbols, and beliefs proves to be a major frustration in missionary efforts and particularly in attempts at conscious establishment of separate institutional units. The mind and spirit of the frontier man and woman can be

captured and placed in a rigid, dogmatic domicile or it can be led
to a deep level of consciousness and spirituality—more often
than not—through an emotional experience.

On the other hand, too, the fact that the Congregational
churches find their distinction in not being distinctive,[26] in terms
of creedal formulations and spiritual journeys, vis-à-vis emotional appeal, can prove to be a major disability in the presenta-
tion of the spirit or image of that denomination to marginal people
who inhabit the frontier.

The Spirit of Congregationalism and
the Visible Signs of Grace

This strong emphasis on covenant, regeneration, or the visible
signs of an invisible grace, rather than on consent to a creed, had
another far-reaching consequence upon the formation of the Congregational spirit. It led to a strong, practical emphasis in theology, ethics, and the practice of ministry. This conception of
church membership and the Christian life drew the line between
Christian and non-Christian upon the basis of visible signs of
redemption evidenced in works as an expression of belief. "By
their works shall the faithful be known" was the notion that
resulted from this conception.

> It was not a matter of church membership or form of
> belief, but of actual change wrought in [people] by the
> power of God. . . . Limited as this method was in its
> application and dependent as it was upon subjective fac-
> tors, it was still practical and realistic in intent. . . . The
> emotional element was inevitably strong, but moral real-
> ity was insisted upon; this, after all, was the basis of
> Puritanism.[27]

In relation to the response of Congregationalism to new frontiers, this strong practical emphasis that drew Puritan insistence
upon tangible expressions of the visitation of God's grace in personal experience had basically two effects. First, Congregationalism was constantly eager to find new situations in which to minister, so that it could visibly prove itself as a community of the
regenerate. As a result, Congregational missionary enterprises
have been numerous and strong. Second, once on the frontier, it

became a prerequisite that all would-be converts to Congregationalism should likewise evidence a strong personal morality and
become alive to issues of social righteousness.[28] Upon the converts to Congregationalism there is placed the imperative for personal morality and an obligation to serve as an integral part of
God's colony in the human world. Because the Congregationalist
and the Congregationalist convert have a strong sense of being
set apart as chosen people in the process of world redemption,
there frequently occurs the illusion that the reward for this task is
a worldly prestige rather than deeper spiritual awareness and
more-responsible freedom.

The Spirit of Congregationalism and the Theocratic Ideal

It would seem, however, that the idea which loomed most large
in the minds of the early Congregationalists, and the moving
force which prevailed in its relation to the Afro-American frontier, was that of establishing a theocratic society governed by the
will of God. As Matthew Spinka indicates,

> Whatever else actuated the leaders of the New England
> colonies in coming to America . . . the purpose of estab-
> lishing a "holy commonwealth" or Kingdom of God,
> was certainly among them. They were willing to settle in
> the American wilderness because they were able to set
> up a form of society, both ecclesiastical and civil, in
> accordance with their understanding of the will of God.
> It was a theocracy at which they aimed—a society gov-
> erned by the will of God expressed in [God's] Word.[29]

There is a certain dynamic involved in the theocratic ideal.
Those who strongly adhere to it cannot rest until the redemption
of the whole society is an accomplished fact. Zealous missionary
endeavors accrue from this conception of the task of the church
or the divinely appointed community. In this respect Congregationalism stood ready to enter the new frontier with great enthusiasm. Its strong passion was the redemption of the whole world, to
transform all heathen or pagan cultures and to establish a society
under God.

But there is an inherent danger in any attempt to establish a theocracy. Theocratization always leads to the establishment and sanction of a particular cultural milieu or social relativity, as if this relativity were absolute and divine. Does this not explain why in the early Puritan colonies only church members received the franchise and why dissent was treated with such rigidity?[30] Rigidity, impatience, and intolerance undergird any human attempt to establish a theocratic society, and when that society moves to a new frontier it feels justified in imposing its own beliefs and way of life upon that new religion or culture. This intransigence prevailed precisely because such a society was convinced that no other culture, faith, belief, or "kind of people" can claim legitimate worth and sanction equal to or above its own. For this reason, then, it has been a historical shortsightedness of American Congregationalism that it has neither fully appreciated nor clearly discerned the value of other life-styles—as over against its confessional liberalism.

Chapter 3

"The Time Has Come"

> Now it was not only evident that God had been educating [the] people in the churches to a larger and better comprehension of their duty to the oppressed, so that when [God's] clock struck the hour for their decision they were ready for the question, but it was also manifest how in the experience of its years the Association had been unconsciously prepared to enter upon a service, the magnitude and opportunity of which would have staggered its faith, had not its previous history made it ready to confront the new problem full of promise and the new work full of grandeur.
>
> —Augustus Field Beard
> *A Crusade of Brotherhood*

Clifton E. Olmstead observes:

> The New England Puritan was always something of an optimist. He believed that God had chosen him to build in the New World a redeemed society. Theoretically, this society extended to the Indians [and later to the Negro], who were considered ideal prospects for mass conversion. The charter of the Massachusetts Bay Colony . . . depicted an Indian crying, "Come over and help us."[1]

Even at this early time the Puritans were concerned with the conversion and transformation of a people and culture that bordered and impinged upon its own. Only with this concern could they consider themselves faithful to their task of being the church. It was not until the nineteenth century, however, that a frontier of a similar yet more intense variety developed around the controversial issue of slavery. In response to this issue, the

American Missionary Association, whose existence achieved ultimate justification through this involvement, came into being.

The association was formed as a residual committee of abolitionists who came to the defense of Africans of the slave ship *Amistad*, who had mutinied, killed the captain, and taken full charge of the ship off the coast of Cuba in 1839. Because of the support of this committee of abolitionists—known as the Amistad Committee—the case reached the Supreme Court of the United States. Former President John Q. Adams, attorney for the defense, pleaded the case eloquently and won their freedom. These Africans of the slave ship *Amistad* returned to their native land, Sierra Leone, West Africa, as free men in 1841.[2]

The Amistad Committee merged with three other antislavery societies at a meeting at Syracuse, New York on September 3, 1846,[3] the Union Missionary Society, the Committee for West Indian Missions, and the Western Evangelical Missionary Society for Work Among the American Indians. These antislavery societies impressed upon the conscience of the nation that "the time has come when those who would sustain missions for the propagation of a pure and free Christianity should institute arrangements for gathering and sustaining churches in heathen lands from which the sins of caste, polygamy, slave-holding and the like should be excluded."[4]

In 1847 in Albany, New York, the American Missionary Association was constitutionally established as an independent nonsectarian organization committed to the "removal of caste wherever its sins are found." The association was both a foreign and a home missionary society. Its foreign field included the Mendi Mission in Sierra Leone, West Africa and missions in Jamaica, Siam, Egypt, the Sandwich Islands, and Canada. Its ministry among the North American Indians was also considered a part of its foreign field. The Home Mission Department embraced two distinct fields: the western United States and the southern United States. By 1860 there were 112 home missionaries employed by the association. Nearly 15 percent were located in the slave states and in Kansas, where they ministered to southern whites. Thus, "the AMA has the distinction of having made the first decided efforts while slavery existed to organize churches and schools for whites in the South on an avowedly anti-slavery basis."[5]

At the opening of the slaveholder's rebellion the Association found itself singularly prepared to devote its energies mainly to the colored race. It had gone through a fifteen year struggle against the terrible power of slavery, North and South, in Church and State, in social and business life, thus bringing it into close sympathy with the oppressed. . . . Moreover it had relinquished . . . nearly all of its missions among the North-Western Indians, while its stations in Siam and the Sandwich Islands had become well nigh self-supporting. Accordingly, when the work of emancipation began, the Association was the first to meet the little bands of escaping slaves with clothing, schools, and the Gospel of Christ, and, by a noteworthy ordering of Providence, its first school* was established at Fortress Monroe, Virginia, near the spot where the first slaveship landed its cargo [†] on the Continent—the slaveship and the colored school marking the two great eras in the history of the Southern States; the one inaugurating that system which blighted the South with the curse of unrequited toil, and desolated the whole land with the miseries of civil war; the other opening the prospect of rewarded industry, universal liberty, general education, freedom of speech and an unfettered Gospel.[6]

The work at Fortress Monroe did not commence, however, until correspondence with General Butler of the Union army was initiated by an officer of the association on August 8, 1861, "with a vein to supplying the physical and general wants of the contrabands."[7] The AMA received its most productive reply from the army from the Rev. P. Franklin Jones, chaplain of one of the New York Regiments of Volunteers, postmarked Camp Butler, Newport News, Virginia, August 21, 1861. It was addressed to the Young Men's Christian Association of the City of New York,

---

*On September 17, 1861 the AMA established the first day school among Freedmen at Fortress Monroe, Virginia. This school laid the foundation for Hampton Institute, which the association founded in 1868 and which was the forerunner of the hundreds of schools that followed.

[†] At Jamestown, Virginia in 1619.

"urging upon them the employment of a missionary to labor among the slaves that had been liberated in Virginia."[8]

The letter was delivered by the Rev. L.C. Lockwood, who had been employed by the Young Men's Christian Association of New York and who was "strongly recommended" to the AMA for the new southern work. "It was deemed best to employ him to visit Fortress Monroe, to make the needful investigation and report to the Committee."[9] Lockwood first visited Washington, D.C., and was "favorably received" by the "members of Government." "In the absence of the Secretary of War, the Assistant Secretary approved the object and recommended him to General Wool who received him cordially and heartily, accepted the view and plan, and afforded him the needful facilities."[10] By November 1861 there were approximately 1,800 Black people at Fortress Monroe, about 600 of whom were children and youth. Lockwood, the first missionary of the association on this new frontier, was busily at work among them.

The fitness of the American Missionary Association for this special work on the new frontier was soon recognized by the churches of the North. The AMA from the beginning was an interdenominational, nonsectarian organization. From the outset the Wesleyan Methodists had given support, and the Freewill Baptists also entered into cooperation with it. In 1866 the Synod of the Reformed Church (Dutch) commended the association as the "instrumentality for schools among the freedmen."[11] Presbyteries and individual Presbyterian churches accepted the association for the same purpose, as did the Reformed Presbyterian churches.[12] It also received endorsement and liberal contributions from Congregationalists of England and Wales, from the Presbyterians of Scotland, and from religious bodies and individuals on the Continent. Owing in part to this generous support, the AMA's receipts, which for the year preceding the rebellion were $43,000, reached $344,500 in cash, besides nearly $90,000 worth of clothing and supplies in 1867. In 1869 its benevolent receipts ranked second only to those of the American Board of Commissioners for Foreign Missions among the ten most-productive and outstanding missionary societies in America.[13]

The events of the war cannot be recounted here, though it could be a significant rehearsal to recite the victories and defeats;

advances and retreats; call after call for hundreds of thousands of soldiers to fill the depleted ranks; the Emancipation Proclamation; the enlistment of the Negro; and, after four tragic but heroic and crucial years, the surrender at Appomattox (1865) and the assassination in Washington. During all this time,

> meeting the advance of the Union Armies . . . thousands of poor illiterate freedmen, in hundreds of AMA schools, plodded patiently through their simple lesson in spelling book and Bible and tried to fit themselves for freedom. The Association gradually withdrew from its home missionary work in the West and gave up most of its foreign work and concentrated [upon work among the Freedmen].[14]

Although the American Missionary Association was interdenominational and constitutionally nonsectarian in character, it was (in terms of the image we have tried to document earlier) Congregational in spirit from the start. Of course, the Congregational churches were major contributors to the AMA. Most of the persons who formed the Amistad Committee and who later constituted the association were Congregationalists. More and more it gathered to itself the leading Congregational ministers and churches.

The first official national meeting of the AMA was at Fourth Congregational Church in Hartford, Connecticut in 1848. Most of its annual meetings thereafter were in Congregational churches. The preachers of annual sermons were usually outstanding Congregationalists, for example, Henry Ward Beecher and Washington Gladden. More than four fifths of the association's presidents were Congregational ministers and lay people. Many notable Congregationalists constituted the roster of its executive committee. Moreover, Congregationalists were outstanding and forceful leaders in the abolitionist movement, of which the association was at the forefront in the North several years before the war. Recounting the events of the New England Reunion of Abolitionists, which met in June 1864, the *American Missionary* reports:

> It was interesting to note what a preponderance there was of the denominational descendents of the Pilgrims among the old Abolitionists. . . . No one could have shied a stick into that crowd without hitting a Congrega-

tionalist, and the chances were three out of four they would have been found to be a Congregational minister at that. . . . In most of the biographical sketches read [at the meeting] it came out that the subject was either a Congregational minister himself or the son of such a minister.[15]

It would appear, then, that a "Congregationalist, by virtue of his ecclesiastical lineage, ought to . . . [have been] a friend of freedom."[16]

Although the association—as we have noted above—had, since its beginning in 1847, depended largely upon Congregational churches and associations for its support, it was not until mid-1864 that it made organized efforts to establish a more permanent relation with them. In that year the association was "represented by one of its Secretaries, or Agents, in all but one of the Meetings of the state Associations and Conferences of the Congregational churches."[17] Resolutions were adopted by "nearly if not quite all" the conferences and associations, and the AMA was "commended to the favor and patronage of the churches, especially with response to the work to which it . . . [had] been providentially called, and in which it . . . [was] largely engaged in the South."[18]

As other denominations withdrew to form their own missionary agencies, the association was left completely in the hands of Congregationalists.[19]

The year 1865 was not only important in the history of the nation, it was also a significant year in the life of the American Missionary Association. It was marked by the close of the Civil War, the establishment of the Freedmen's Bureau by an act of Congress, and the convening of the National Council of Congregational Churches in Boston. At this meeting the council recommended that the churches raise $250,000 for work among Freedmen and designated the AMA as the organization "providentially fitted to carry it forward." The association accepted the responsibility and appointed district secretaries at Chicago, Cincinnati, and Boston and collecting agents in other areas of the northern states. In that year it succeeded in securing more than the $250,000 recommended by the Congregational council. As a result of such continuing support from the ranks of Congregationalism, its receipts rose from $47,828 in 1861 to $253,045 in 1866 and $420,768 by 1870.[20]

It is true, of course, that the AMA did not officially become an agency of the Congregational churches until the meeting of the National Council of Congregational Churches in 1913.[21] At this meeting the association, along with other Congregational boards, came into the council and under its control. We cannot, however, escape the fact that even initially the association was almost totally Congregational in its personnel, financial support, and control. What is more important, we cannot either escape the fact that the association was always Congregational in spirit and orientation. The heritage, myths, images, dynamic patterns, and religious and cultural ideals of this denomination were in very few respects unlike those of the denomination itself. Even the association's nonsectarian principle was a part of the Congregational Way. How could any organization so integrally related to the Puritan tradition be otherwise? For the Congregational churches, the New England ethos and the association were all products of the Pilgrim and Puritan mind. The image they had of themselves and their conception of the vocation they were to fulfill in society were identical.

This deep kinship of the AMA with Congregationalism becomes more clear when one looks at its relationship with and responsibilities to other contributing denominations and compares this with its relationship and responsibilities to the Congregational churches. The relationship with other denominations was, on the whole, a functional one. For the Freewill Baptists, cooperation pertained mainly to governmental facilities. The Reformed Church and individual New School Presbyterian churches and other religious bodies selected the association to be merely their administrator of funds for the education of Freedmen and a channel for physical relief. For those churches the AMA endeavored only to take the teachers they commended to them, to locate them where they could be of the most benefit to Black people, and to be as "helpful" as possible to the home missions these churches had in the South.

The relationship of the AMA with the Congregational churches, on the other hand, was more organic; it was "spiritual" and "church-forming." Of all the denominations, it was the Congregational churches alone that commissioned the association to serve the Freedmen, not only through schools and physical relief but through ministers and missionaries of the gospel as well. In response to this commission, the association did all it could with the means entrusted to it to relieve want, maintain Christian schools, and plan, plant, and nourish churches of the faith and order of the Puritan fathers.[22] No denomination or religious movement is more daring than when it entrusts its life and mission—its faith and order—to an agent whose image, aspirations, beliefs, and spirit are alien to its own. Hence the intimate wedding of these two organizations was in no sense accidental. Both the association and the denomination felt that

> the permanent duty of the nation, and especially the churches, to the emancipated slaves . . . [was] to fit them for their new positions as citizens, and their true destiny as [people] and Christians in America, and as missionaries to Africa. . . . [They believed that] no Christian church. . . [could] discharge its duty to them by merely denominationalizing them into its ranks, leaving the essentials of character and Christian [personhood] unchanged.[23]

Because of the deep religious and cultural kinship of the American Missionary Association and Congregationalism, it is almost unnecessary to say that the "essentials of character and Christian" personhood as here conceived found exemplars among the ranks of the New England middle class and particularly among those of the Congregational "bourgeois type of religious faith."

The meaning of this common culture and ethos needs further elaboration. It can be noted that, when social patterns are observed, American churches in their origin and continuance have been more often than not influenced by class and provincial consideration than by a common commitment of faith.[24] To the degree that the spirit of Congregationalism had permeated the whole of New England society, therefore, this Spirit facilitated also the development and transmission of distinctive cultural, social, economic, and political norms as well. On the new southern frontier this same generative force was at work in the social and cultural patterns of the communities in which the AMA did its work.[25]

Thus, while the social situation of the New England Congregationalist and the newly emancipated Negro were by no stretch of
the imagination akin, in order for Congregationalism to establish
itself among people whose circumstance was so widely divergent
from its own, a common denominator or meeting ground had to
be laid. This common meeting ground would be a means whereby
the Afro-American was brought to that level of intelligence, character, Christian personhood, emotional sobriety, and economic
and social sufficiency in keeping with the Congregational image
and ideal. The channel through which the Freedman was to become "fit" for the church and the world—theocratically conceived—was a school thoroughly enmeshed in a Congregational
and New England persuasion. In this process the schools and
churches started by the AMA were not merely instruments for
the establishment of religious norms in any narrow sense. They
were also the instruments for the nurture of a complex subculture
relevant to all phases of human existence.[26]

Indeed, the establishment of the spirit of Congregationalism in
its most pure form was the intention of the early missionaries of
the association who ventured into the Black South. Yet, it must
be noted that there were signs of distortion of this spirit and ideal,
even at an early point in time. Those who were charged with the
responsibility of sharing the Pilgrim heritage with the Freedmen
became impatient with persons whose life-styles, economic status, religious expression, and intellectual modes were unlike their
own. Those who were charged with the responsibility of sharing
this heritage sought to impose the Congregational spirit as if it
were absolute and divine.

Chapter 4
"Awaiting New Wonders"

There seems to be more of a religious element in the character of the Negroes upon some plantations than others, owing perhaps to the different influences to which they have been subjected, both before and since the rebellion. Here this element greatly prevails, and meetings are held two or three times on the Sabbath, and on every alternate evening during the week. On the Sabbath morning, (the Praise House being near by) we are awakened at half-past four by the ringing of a bell, and a half-hour later we listen to songs of praise—for these houses of praise are rightly named, their religious exercises consisting mostly of singing. And sweet to us is the dawn of the Sabbath-day ushered in by the rich melody of their voices, as they sing the time honored tunes, which recall to our minds the home-circle and prayer-meeting. Yet these poor people are as sheep without a shepherd, and sadly need an instructor in the Divine life, to teach them that religion is not all an emotional feeling, but must be daily practiced in their lives. This truth we endeavor to impress upon the minds of the children, both in the Sabbath and day schools; at the former the adults are frequently among our most attentive listeners. Oh, how often I long for that spirit which used to descend in olden times, upon the young men and young women, that I may edify their famishing souls.

—Carolyn E. Jocelyn
American Missionary, 1869

Long before the American Missionary Association had gone south with the school, the gospel, and the New England-Congregational Way, Christianity had become a vital force and tradition among the enslaved. Americans of African descent go as far back in the history of the New World as any of the various ethnic groups. Blacks may have sailed with Columbus on his voyages to the Western World. It is certain that Blacks accompanied Balboa, Cortés, Ayllon, Pizarro, De Soto, Valdivia, and other Spanish explorers to the Americas. The history of the settling of Blacks in the United States, however, begins with the landing of twenty Africans from a Dutch ship at Jamestown, Virginia in August 1619. This was more than a year before the Pilgrim fathers set foot on Plymouth Rock.

The census of 1790 (the first census of the United States) reports that there were approximately 700,000 Black slaves and nearly 60,000 free Blacks in the United States when the count was taken. As would be assumed, almost all free Negroes lived north of the Mason-Dixon line and almost all the slaves lived south of it. At the outbreak of the War Between the States there were approximately 4,000,000 slaves and 500,000 Negroes who were free. Of this total number of Blacks, it is believed that only twenty had received a college education since they had first arrived as slaves and indentured servants in 1619. It is important to note that at the time of the census of 1790 an estimated one out of every six Blacks professed the Christian faith.[1]

Despite this relatively small proportion of Black Christians, the church was by far the most significant and firmly established institution among the enslaved, and it had become particularized in accordance with the peculiar history and circumstances that surrounded and resulted from the institution and ethos of bondage and subservience.

Congregationalism was a name and church unknown and unheard of by antebellum Blacks. To be sure, they had never dreamed that there was a society "this South-hell-ward of Heaven" of such wealth, intellect, culture, and freedom as that maintained by the New England established middle class of the Congregational Way. The American Missionary Association, therefore, firmly enmeshed in the New England Congregational tradition, encompassed a social and religious orientation that was alien—or at best strange—to the Black South. Surely it would be greeted with trepidation rather than enthusiasm and "cheer."[2]

But the greatest obstacle or opposing force that the association faced in its effort to establish Congregational churches on the new southern frontier was not simply that opposition which inevitably confronts all things unfamiliar and new. It encountered a resistance and a contempt that was far more formidable and intense. This opposing force was the strength of the already profoundly entrenched Black church tradition that could be neither easily flouted nor broken through. When the Congregational tradition of New England—led by the theocratic spirit to transform —encountered the Afro-American church tradition of the agricultural proslavery South, a simple victory through education, evangelization, and "friendly missionary persuasion" could not be assured. Here were two stubborn, dynamic church movements, produced and continued by extremely divergent social, racial, and religious histories, and with various concepts of what the church and society are and should be. The patient but persistent struggle of Congregationalism to establish churches among Blacks in the South can neither be appreciated nor fully understood, save in the light of the significance of its confrontation with this dynamic tradition, the Black church, which—going back even to its far-off African past—met and resisted it with remarkable strength.

There have been many attempts to understand and explain the peculiarities of the Black church as it existed prior to and just after the Civil War. Most of these attempts, however, end in self-defeat unless it is recognized that any such attempt must always be relative and incomplete. A great deal may be said by way of interpretation that the church of the Afro-American was originally part and parcel of the dynamic which characterizes any religious movement of the untutored and the socially and economically disfranchised class. For example, H. Richard Niebuhr has suggested that the distinct ethical and psychological characteristics of such movements correspond to the constituent's educational, economic, and social development.

> Emotional fervor is one common mark. When the power
> of abstract thought has not been highly developed . . .
> religion must and will express itself in emotional terms.
> . . . Ethically, as well as psychologically, such religion
> bears a distinct character. The salvation which it seeks
> and sets forth is the salvation of the disinherited. Intel-

lectual naivete and practical need combine to create a marked propensity toward millenarianism with its promise of tangible goods and of reversal of all present social systems of rank.[3]

In significant measure, Niebuhr's interpretation of church movements of the lower strata provides the larger framework in which the Black church tradition can be understood. But further interpretation is needed if we are to supply the more necessary details.

One is sorely tempted simply to indicate the historical causes of the Afro-American Christian movement and to apply the implications of "pure" historical fact within the context of our present task. In so doing we could suggest several events in the American church tradition which brought Afro-Americans into Christianity and which account, in part, for the racial bifurcation of the American Protestant Church.[4] But a complete interpretation of the peculiar character of the Black Christian movement prior to the Civil War cannot be found within a general history of Protestantism in the United States.

On the other hand, it is unfortunate that the early Afro-American church movement has little written history to which an interpreter may confidently turn.[5] Although the frequent solution to this dilemma has been to turn to the general history of Protestantism in America and to discover from it how the Black church came to be, this approach precludes the significant inner history of the Black church—a history peculiar to itself.

It would be a bold but inadequate interpretation to suggest that the church of the Negroes was a religious movement or institution imposed on them by the American Protestant church at large. One must indicate that Christianity became a dynamic movement and firm tradition in the inner history and distinctive social patterns of Black life itself.

In the first place, one could account for the evangelistic and revivalistic character of the Black church tradition by pointing to the fact that a great many slaves were converted to the faith during the first and second Great Awakenings of the eighteenth and nineteenth centuries. This evangelical fervor and emotional expression of Christianity was that which Blacks first and most thoroughly knew. To this brand of Christianity, therefore, there was continued attachment. Certainly it is true that the emotionalism of the Methodist and Baptist itinerant ministers who possessed the southern frontier contributed greatly to the shaping of the pattern of Christian expression and laid authoritative claims upon the Black religion, with which formatively they had so much to do. Yet, it must be said that the mass conversion of Blacks in the Great Awakening periods and the emotional appeal of the Methodist and Baptist itinerants would have had little if any effect upon Afro-American religious modes had there not been a strong affinity between these revival movements and an indigenous religious dynamic already present and at work in antebellum Black life.

The original or native social environment of Blacks in America was the "polygamous clan life under the potent influence of the priest. His religion was nature worship, with profound belief in invisible surrounding influences, good and bad, and his worship was through mystery and sacrifice."[6] The religion of the slave, therefore, was rooted from the beginning in the mysterious, emotional disciplines of primitive cultic rites. Emotive, esoteric rites were part and parcel of Black culture and life.

An instructive glimpse of the feedback of the African clan life upon the New World experience of the Black person is incisively rendered by W.E.B. DuBois in the following terms: There were several

> rude changes in the Negro's pattern of life which influenced and increased the emotive dimension of his religious expression. Not least among these were the traumatic experience of being removed from the homeland, the long gruesome voyage on the slave ship, and—for some—the hard labor and regimentation in West-Indian sugar fields. But beside geographical or physical dislocation, the Negro's entire social pattern and emotional or psychological orientation were disrupted and abruptly changed. Indeed, the slave was the uprooted—the displaced. In the search for identity, a "homeland" or a feeling of "oneness" in a radically different and new province, the plantation replaced the clan and the tribe . . . the white master replaced the chief, [and] the old ties of blood relationship and kinship disappeared, and instead of the family appeared a new polygamy and

33

polyandry, which, in some cases, bordered on promiscuity.[7]

In the midst of this traumatic social disruption and painful, revolutionary change, the Black slave—in an effort to adjust—retained a vestige of the former social and religious arrangement, and

the chief remaining institution was the priest or medicine man. He early appeared on the plantation and found his function as the healer of the sick, the interpreter of the unknown, the comforter of the sorrowing, the supernatural avenger of wrong, and the one who rudely but picturesquely expressed the longing, disappointment, and the resentment of a stolen oppressed people. Thus, as bard, physician, judge and priest, within the narrow limits allowed by the slave system, rose the Negro preacher, and under him the first Afro-American institution, the Negro Church.[8]

This religious movement was a product of African and slave life—a dynamic force essentially independent from the American Protestant church. It was "an adaptation and mingling of heathen rites among the members of each plantation and roughly designated as Voodooism."[9]

In a study entitled *Voodoo in Haiti*, Alfred Métraux, one of the most distinguished ethnologists of the twentieth century, discusses African and Christian religious beliefs and practices that came together to form voodoo. Métraux's findings shed light on our concerns, for as an outgrowth of his study he concludes that voodoo is

nothing more than a conglomeration of beliefs and rites of African origin, which, having been closely unified with Catholic practice, has come to be the religion of the greater part of the peasants and the urban proletariat of the Black republic of Haiti. Its devotees ask of it what [people] have always asked of religion: remedy for ills, satisfaction of needs and hope of survival.[10]

Similarly, it is our belief that Black religion in America is inevitably a conglomeration of beliefs and rites of African origin that, having been mixed with practices of evangelical Protestantism, has come to be the basis of the religion of the greater portion of

Blacks in America. Indeed, it may be reasserted with confidence that, as with the interlocking influences of the religion of Haiti, so devotees of Black religion in America "ask of it what [people] have always asked of any religion: remedy for ills, satisfaction of needs . . . hope of survival" and, of course, a deeper consciousness of spiritual realities. It would seem, then, that the primary mission of the American churches to the freshly imported Negro slaves consisted largely in providing Protestant Christian content and categories and a specific ongoing religious history and tradition through which the religious dynamic peculiar to the slave and bequeathed out of the slave's past could be authentically conceptualized through the familiar and acceptable symbols of the American Protestant church tradition—Black religion could be viscerally expressed. The Black church tradition, therefore, as it gradually became Christian, was a peculiar complex of the African religious spirit and an evangelical, revivalistic faith of American Protestantism as this blend was appropriated by a thoroughly disinherited class.[11]

Second, in the early Afro-American church tradition a direct relationship between the Christian "religion" and a Western Christian ethic was never fully established. The disruption of monogamous family life and "forced"—or, at best, condoned promiscuity—were economically advantageous to a productive slave enterprise. Families had to be intentionally produced out of the bonds of wedlock. They had to be broken for the expedient and profitable sale of slaves. Cohabitation and "scientific breeding" were accepted practices of the trade. Since it was essential to the endurance and financial solvency of the slave market that Blacks become both "passively" Christian and sexually "immoral," the essential relationship between Christian religion and Western morals could not be profitably maintained.

Thus, the fact that Blacks were "given" a religion and Christianity while at the same time denied freedom to exercise moral responsibility is most significant in determining the practices and emphasis of the early Black church tradition.

Further, since there was no stable political communal or family life among Blacks the church was the only available institution wherein that which had been uniquely the Black's social and religious experience in America could be preserved. This fact stands out in remarkable relief, since segregation of the races in American churches had not always been the practice. Before the Civil War—in both the North and the South—Blacks and whites worshiped in the same churches, although Blacks sat in the galleries and the "separate cup of the One Body and Blood" was widely in use. But the fact that slave and master worshiped in common sanctuaries seldom if ever meant that there existed between whites and Blacks a fully identical religious and social commonality in which all persons are united and spiritually at one. When, therefore, there was a realistic prospect that the slave system would end, the Black's "church within the church" was the appropriate institution in which that which was the Black person's very own could be faithfully preserved. Within the context of their own peculiar religious experiences, Blacks could structure and express a response to the challenge of the experience that lay ahead.

These independent churches were the first organizational enterprises of Blacks in America. They became the institutional embodiment of a socio-religious tradition in which Afro-Americans could develop a sense of mooring for individuals as well as for the group. The Black church was truly the Black person's sanctuary. It was the Black's homeland, the Black's "nation," in an alien and hostile land. In the Black church the Negro could fathom the depths and meaning of the Black's strange past and could find in the fellowship with kindred souls a hope and channel for the future.

Finally, the religion of the slave tradition was greatly influenced by the Black's passionate and incessant desire to be free. Particularly at the beginning of the nineteenth century, when the social and religious forces in the nation began to exert upon the slave system revolutionary pressures that would eventually bring abolition, Afro-Americans—especially those who were free—discerned the signs of the changing time and knew that emancipation was a future but certain reality. Even within American Protestantism the controversial issue of slavery created an unrest that resulted in several denominational splits between the churches of the North and the South. When the Methodists divided in 1844, the Baptists in 1845, and the Presbyterians in 1861, the Afro-American was the least perturbed. These schisms were counted as "moments of reckoning" that would hasten the day when the Blacks would, at last, be free.

> Through fugitive slave and irrepressible discussion, . . . [the] desire for freedom seized the black millions still in bondage, and became their one ideal of life. . . . Negro religion thus transformed itself with the dream of abolition, until that which was a radical fad in the white North and an anarchistic plot in the white South had become a religion in the black world.[12]

When the

> war was over and the Negro had been freed, the expression of the most fundamental human emotions could no longer be interfered with. Parents would no longer be torn from their children or children from their parents; women would no longer be outraged almost before the very eyes of their husbands and fathers. To this there was no difficulty for the people to adjust themselves. No new problem was involved here. But new situations arose to which adjustment was absolutely imperative. How were they to support themselves in this inimical environment?[13]

Negroes received emancipation with mixed emotions. On the one hand, at last they were free. W.E.B. DuBois puts it poetically:

> When emancipation finally came, it seemed to the freedman a literal coming of the Lord. His fervid imagination was stirred as never before, by the tramp of armies, the blood and dust of battles, and the wail and whirl of social upheaval. He stood dumb and motionless before the whirlwind: What would he do with it? Was it not the Lord's doing, and marvelous in his eyes? Joyed and bewildered as he was with what came, he stood awaiting new wonders.[14]

On the other hand, freedom brought with it a demand for a total restructuring of all previous social and psychological orderings of their lives. All the social patterns that Black people had known as slaves were now disrupted. They could not immediately fathom the responsible but uncertain life of the free. Almost overnight they had been cast into a totally unfamiliar dimension of freedom and existence by which they were threatened and which left them painfully insecure. How could they bring order and harmony into this wonderfully frightful chaos? There was no equanimity for a people faced on all sides by insecurity, doubt, and threat of personal disintegration.[15]

Perhaps it was only in such a transitional setting as this that the Black person's conversion experience could confirm its own power, its own radical capacity to impose a climate, an irreversible freedom, which no formal proclamation could even remotely convey.

Chapter 5
"Broad and Deep Foundations"

The Pilgrims laid broad and deep foundations, in addition to leading upright lives. They established the church and school by the side of the civil state. They opened the school to the children of the community without exception, that education might be universal. They made the church democratic and what we call Congregational in polity. They thus infused the spirit of intelligence and of liberty into the entire population. Every church was a cradle of liberty, every school was a nurse of patriots. The South had never had a common school system. Slavery forbade it. Congregationalism could gain no foothold in that region, and for the same reason.

—William W. Patton
Journal of Negro Education

At its inception, the American Missionary Association was not primarily an educational society. It was an agency for missionary endeavor and was organized primarily to extend the gospel. The very first issue of the *American Missionary* (October 1859) states: "Its field is unrestricted: it is the world. Beginning at our own highly favored and guilty country, it will, as it is able, preach the Gospel to the poor, assist feeble churches, sustain missionary operation amongst the free colored population and preach deliverance to the crushed and stricken slave."[1]

Writing in the Summer 1960 edition of the *Journal of Negro Education*, Wesley A. Hotchkiss, executive secretary of the American Missionary Association, observes that very early in the life of the association, which was then a worldwide society, "it clarified to itself all of the far-reaching and revolutionary implications of its slogan: 'Equal brotherhood in the family of Christ.'" This slogan became its "doctrine of man" and formed the rock upon which its educational structure was erected. Hotchkiss says further that "in retrospect, it seems providential that the AMA should have come to its educational task among Negro Americans through this route. The transcendent power of this philosophical base for education was able to withstand all the hostilities directed against it."[2] Since the propagation of the gospel was this "philosophical base" upon which the American Missionary Association was founded, the AMA schools were a means to that end. These schools became an expression of the mission of the association, but they were never regarded as ends in themselves. As late as 1877 an author writing in the *American Missionary* said of the association's educational task: "Knowledge, merely acquired, has no saving grace: only as it is digested, assimilated, worked into daily life, forming habits, sustaining principles, creating sentiment, is it power for good. Till then it may be a dangerous thing."[3] We can conclude, therefore, that the "AMA was not organized as an educational society and all its later efforts would be misunderstood if these underlying motives were not recognized."[4]

The "far-reaching and revolutionary implications" of the association's slogan, "Equal brotherhood in the family of Christ," must be spelled out even further. In the preceding chapters as we discussed the spirit of Congregationalism we attempted to make several points clear: (1) For New England Congregationalists the whole of society was to be ordered under God. Theirs was basically a theocracy, not a democracy. (2) Because of their confusion of a "pure theocracy" with a social, economic, and intellectual style of life peculiar to the New England established middle class, even with the greatest effort it was difficult for them not to regard the Congregational Way as absolute and divine. (3) The AMA, because of its deep spiritual and functional kinship with Congregationalism, was likewise caught up in the problem of assessing the relationship of Christ and culture. (4) To the extent that the association felt as did the Congregationalists that God in Christ is best revealed in a particular kind of culture or ethos, it determined as a missionary society to prepare the emancipated slave through education and moral and cultural elevation for Christ and church most clearly revealed in the New England Congregational Way. This could only be accomplished as it broke through the Black socio-religious tradition—a soil upon which Congregationalism could not easily feed.

The association and the denomination felt, therefore, that their goal could be attained only through an extensive program of education, which would prepare Freedmen—who were of a peculiar religion, culture, and past—for responsible membership in Congregational churches and for free citizenship in a theocratic society. Hence, the schools preceded the church and were to function as auxiliaries of the church. Not only was the slogan "Equal brotherhood in the family of Christ" a democratic ideal that could be achieved by secular education for citizenship in a democratic society, but it was also theocratic, and its ultimate attainment could be reached only when people professed this kinship in the Congregational kind of expression of the church of Christ.

With the opening of the first shanty school at Fortress Monroe, Virginia on September 17, 1861, the process of "education and acculturation for Christianization" was begun. "Mrs. Mary Peake, a frail little Negro woman [a mulatto] who had been educated by a wealthy plantation family, began by assembling a group of twenty scholars to teach [the Freedmen] to read and write and to love God."[5] From this humble beginning of one missionary (L.C. Lockwood), one teacher (Mary S. Peake), and twenty pupils—just a fraction of the 1,800 illiterate and semi-illiterate at Fortress Monroe—the work of the association grew markedly. Only a year later, in October 1862, there were eighteen teachers and missionaries, and by July 1863 the number had increased to seventy, eight of whom were Black, either free before the proclamation of emancipation or indigenous to the contraband[6] community.

These Christian missionaries and teachers, largely natives of New England, were laboring in eastern Virginia at Fortress Monroe, Hampton, Croney Island, Yorktown, Portsmouth, Norfolk and vicinity; at Washington, D.C.; in South Carolina at Port Royal, Beaufort and vicinity, Hilton Head, and St. Helena. They were also ministering to the needs of the contrabands at Cairo, Illinois; Columbus, Kentucky; St. Louis, Missouri; Memphis and vicinity, Tennessee; Helena, Arkansas; and Kansas. Besides this zealous activity, letters of request for missionary assistance had been received by the association from several points on the Mississippi River below Vicksburg, specifically from New Orleans. The number of scholars in the weekday schools had reached not fewer than 4,000 (not counting sabbath school enrollment), or 2

41

percent of the 200,000 Blacks who were free at this time. In the four months between July and November 1863 the number of scholars enrolled in the day and night schools had increased nearly twofold, from 4,000 to 7,000 (not counting the 5,000 enrolled in the sabbath schools), and the number of teachers, missionaries, ministers, and assistants had risen from 70 to 102.

A year later, in July 1864, the association was engaged in significant missionary activity in additional locales, including Arlington Heights and Ferry Point, Virginia; Harpers Ferry, West Virginia; New Bern, Beaufort, Morehead City, and Roanoke Island, North Carolina; Nashville, Tennessee; Little Rock, Arkansas; Natchez, Mississippi; and Port Huron, Baton Rouge, and New Orleans, Louisiana. Indeed, the association's largest field was Norfolk, Virginia, where there were 1,200 students in the "regular schools," 1,400 in the sabbath schools, 8 "hopeful conversions," 11 missionaries, 10 Black assistants, and a "mobile unit" that provided religious instruction and schools on four farms cultivated by Freedmen.[7]

Between 1861 and 1871, the first decade of its work on the new frontier, the AMA had spent $2,222,498.83 for the work among Freedmen; had commissioned 3,470 ministers, missionaries, and teachers; and had had a total of 321,099 students enrolled in nearly 350 temporary, or makeshift, schools.[8] The year 1871, the final year of the decade, marked the peak of AMA educational activity, with 21,848 students enrolled in 170 day and night schools, which were now beginning to be firmly, or at least semi-permanently, established.[9]

The trend toward permanent schools began in 1866, the year after the war, as the Black population was actually becoming relatively fixed and fairly predictable as to areas of concentration. During this period of Afro-American community establishment, the AMA began to build permanent schools and teachers' quarters of its own and to purchase tracts of land. At this point the association was gradually beginning to conceive its mission in the South not simply as that of an agency of temporary "war relief" but as that of an institution and movement of permanent "reconstruction, transformation and redemption" as well.[10]

Upon discovering the necessity for permanent institutional establishment,
the leaders of the AMA saw their educational task in

somewhat comprehensive terms: The common schools which [would] spring up in great numbers . . . [would] give way to graded schools; these graded schools . . . [would] take on normal departments with teachers of experience and devotion who [should] prepare their pupils for such instruction as they in turn . . . [might] impart in smaller places. This theory at once made necessary higher institutions with collegiate intention, which should receive exceptional pupils prepared at the secondary schools who were approved and encouraged by their teachers to seek exceptional education. Meanwhile, parochial schools . . . [were to] be continued in connection with the little churches of ignorant people, the teachers working in the churches as well as the schools.[11]

To further meet the demands of this "comprehensive task" of education and evangelization, the original plan of the association was to establish and maintain one college or university in each of the larger states in the South, normal and graded schools in the principal cities, and common or parochial schools in the smaller villages and rural communities. This proposal proved too ambitious, and in the course of time, as the southern states instituted improved and enlarged public education for Blacks, the AMA found it financially and morally expedient in most instances to withdraw support from its secondary, elementary, and college programs. Under the original plan, many outstanding institutions were founded. These schools were relatively permanent and served with distinction in the area of education. Among them were:

District of Columbia

Howard University	Washington

Virginia

Gloucester Normal	Capahosic
Hampton Institute	Hampton

North Carolina

Gregory Normal	Wilmington
Brick Junior College	Brick
(Later: Brick Rural Life School)	
(Later: Franklinton Center at Brick)	

43

Peabody Academy	Troy
Lincoln Academy	Kings Mountain
Washburn Seminary	Beaufort

South Carolina

| Avery Institute | Charleston |

Georgia

Storrs School	Atlanta
Atlanta University	Atlanta
Ballard Normal	Macon
(Formerly Lewis High)	
Beach Institute	Savannah
Allen Normal	Thomasville
Dorchester Academy	McIntosh
(Now Dorchester Center)	

Florida

| Fessenden Academy | Ocala |
| Stanton Institute | Jacksonville |

Alabama

Talladega College	Talladega
Lincoln Normal	Marion
Burrell Normal	Florence
Emerson Institute	Montgomery
Trinity School	Athens
Drewry High School	Talladega

Kentucky

| Chandler Normal | Lexington |
| Berea College | Berea |

Tennessee

LeMoyne-Owen College	Memphis
(Formerly Phoenix and Lincoln Schools)	
Fisk University	Nashville

Texas

| Tillotson | Austin |
| (Now Huston-Tillotson) | |

Arkansas

| Helena Normal | Helena |

Mississippi

| Tougaloo University | Tougaloo |
| (Now Tougaloo Christian College) | |

44

Straight University   New Orleans
   (Now Dillard Christian University)

Of the above-named colleges, Talladega, Fisk, LeMoyne-Owen, Huston-Tillotson, Dillard, and Tougaloo Christian still maintain a relationship with the American Missionary Association.

With this ambitious program of education and with more than a million freed children to educate (requiring at least 20,000 teachers),

> it soon became evident to the AMA that its major task in mass education was to teach the teachers. Accordingly, every school which went on to higher education had a normal [teacher training] department. In many of these, state governments cooperated by making appropriations. The Freedmen's Bureau was also a partner in this enterprise. According to a statistical report in 1873, Fisk University sent out during the year one hundred ten teachers, the six other chartered institutions furnished four hundred fifty, normal and graded schools, one hundred fifty, aggregating seven hundred ten teachers, teaching sixty-four thousand pupils.[12]

Still, only a fraction of the many illiterate were reached.

Throughout all the years of struggle, growth, conquests, and defeat, the schools of the American Missionary Association never lost sight of their dual task of education and evangelization, which for the AMA, because of its religious and cultural heritage, were synonymous functions. That there was this strong conception of the interrelatedness of the church and the school is amply illustrated in the kind of teacher the association sought. On August 25, 1864 the Rev. W.J. Richardson, a missionary at Beaufort, South Carolina, wrote:

> We wish [that] the rule adopted by the American Missionary Association not to commission any teacher who does not possess evangelical faith in Christ, might be kept more prominently before the Northern Churches. We want only teachers who love to point souls to the Lamb of God, as we believe that philanthropy without

faith in the Redeemer is wholly inadequate to the great work of enlightening and Christianizing this people.[13]

To this end, in July 1866 "The Six Qualifications for Missionaries Among the Freedmen" was published in *American Missionary*. The qualifications were a missionary spirit, good health, energy, culture and common sense, good personal habits, and experience.[14] In response to the high calling of this work, one teacher wrote:

> In this consecration—this death to this world—I also made up my mind to accept all that should follow. Imperfect as had been my life, I do not remember that, in all my after difficulties, I had to consider anew the question of property, of comfort or apparel, of personal safety, of giving life itself. The latter I regarded as even probable.[15]

The teachers of the AMA were made aware that "if education does not make for spiritual life and spiritual power, it is lamentably insufficient. Therefore, the Gospel of Christ was to be put into every study, into every science, into every line of thought, and into every form of work."[16]

The teachers and schools were indeed of a strong Christian persuasion and possessed of a deep sense of evangelical vocation, and in a very real sense these teachers and schools *were* the church. Augustus Field Beard indicates that "from the first the school was an embryo church. Every day, Services and Sunday Schools found their home in the school house."[17] The school was a worshiping and learning community. The tasks of the church and the school were functionally commensurate. It can be observed that there was a substantial overlapping of the students who attended the day and night schools and those who came for instruction in and conversion to the faith on the sabbath. For example, in the year 1871 the total number of students enrolled in the day, night, and sabbath schools was 38,102. Of this total, 16,254 of these pupils were enrolled in the sabbath schools alone and instructed in the knowledge and principles of the Christian faith.[18]

Yet a deeper and more intangible sense of identity, transcending statistical verification and functional comparison, was evident as a "spiritual" identity or "at-oneness" between association, church, and school. Each school was a "worshiping-learning community"—indeed, each school was the church. The nature and purpose of each were one and the same. In this dialectic between the function of church and school, the age-old question "What has Athens to do with Jerusalem?" seemed momentarily resolved. In keeping with this idea, Hotchkiss says:

> The philosophy of the first schools was so closely identified with its Christian motivation that they tended toward parochialism. The school was not distinguished from the church, in fact it tended to be a week-long Sunday School. Secretary Beard justifies this tendency as follows: "If emphasis appears to have been placed on the schools it was because they were the foundation for the churches."[19]

The missionaries labored among the Freedmen in an effort to enable them to walk erect as children of God. "Both the Church and the school were involved in this to such an extent that the distinction of the two institutions submerged in the overwhelming magnitude of the task."[20]

We have, then, in this "holy amalgam" a multiple identity of church and school, knowledge and faith, Congregationalism and association, New England-religion-and-culture and the kingdom of God. For these early Congregational-minded missionaries there could be no strict demarcation between Athens and Jerusalem, society and faith. Education and social elevation were commensurate with Christianization. It was the belief of the association that the Afro-American—subject as he was to naïveté, emotionalism, and "immorality" imposed by the abuses of slavery—could not perfectly attain Christian personhood save through the Congregational-New England Way.

But in spite of the human weaknesses that emerged in this work of "devotion" and "consecration," there were redeeming forces through and through. That Blacks were and remained aware and deeply grateful for these "outward signs of an inward grace"—evidenced in the sacrificial labors of myriad Christian teachers of the AMA—is richly spoken by W.E.B. DuBois.

> This was the gift of New England to the freed Negro: not alms, but a friend; not cash but character. . . . The teachers in these institutions came not to keep the Ne-

groes in their place, but to raise them out of the defilement of the places where slavery had wallowed them. The colleges they founded were social settlements; homes where the best of the sons of the freedmen came in close sympathetic touch with the best traditions of New England. They lived and ate together, studied and worked, hoped and harkened in the dawning light. In actual formal content their curriculum was doubtless old-fashioned, but in educational power it was supreme, for it was the contact of living souls.[21]

With its knowledge of culture, education, and religion, the association sought to teach the teachers, to train the preachers, to make a closer union between religion and morals, worship and work, learning and faith. Something of the spirit of the Hebrew prophet, the Puritan preacher, and the Pilgrim moralist came to the South, the land of poetry and song, as an incomplete manifestation of the Body of Christ and to establish a partial and socially peculiar kinship in the "holy commonwealth" among all people.

Chapter 6

"A Controlling Power in a Dark Land"

> The American Missionary Association has been selected
> by two Congregational Councils and by the very general
> acquiescence of the churches to do their work and it has
> begun and carried it forward in the right way. It has
> adopted New England's method, as practiced at home
> and in the West, of planting the pure church, the Chris-
> tian school, and thus laying the foundation for the cul-
> tured home, the useful citizen and the intelligent
> Christian.
>
> *American Missionary*, July 1874

Many years before the American Missionary Association went
south with the Bible and the book, Black people were a part of
the Congregational denomination. The first Black Congregational
church to be formally and separately organized in America was
the Dixwell Avenue Congregational Church in New Haven, Connecticut. Established in 1820, for a time the Dixwell Church stood
alone as the representative of organized Congregationalism
among Blacks in the United States. A few years after the formation of the New Haven church, several others were established in
the North. Among these were the Talcott Street Church in Hartford, Connecticut (established in 1833); the Fourth Congregational Church of Portland, Maine (1843); and the Second Congregational Church of Pittsfield, Massachusetts (1846). By 1847, the
same year that the American Missionary Association was incorporated, there were already six Black Congregational churches
scattered in five states—Connecticut, Massachusetts, Rhode Island, Ohio, and Maine.

Even before the establishment of these northern Black Congregational churches, one had witnessed the nurture within the framework of Congregationalism of a Black man of the accomplishments of Lemuel Haynes. Haynes, a Black soldier in the American Revolution, was a minister of the Congregational churches. The Rev. Haynes was born in 1753 at West Hartford, Connecticut and was the first Black person to receive a college degree and to become an ordained minister in America. In 1785 he became pastor of an all-white Congregational church in Torrington, Connecticut. In 1818 he went to serve a Congregational church in Manchester, New Hampshire, where he made himself famous. He became most widely known for his sermon "Against Universalism," which he preached in opposition to Hosea Ballou, the champion of universalism. This sermon was published and widely circulated in the United States and Europe. Lemuel Haynes, the first Black Congregationalist "man of the cloth" died in Granville, New York in 1832.

Contrary to common belief, there were also Black Congregationalists in the South prior to the Civil War, although they were not organized into separate congregations. Among the earliest records that can be discovered of Blacks entering into the fellowship of Congregationalism are those found at Charleston, South Carolina. The Old Circular Church, a white congregation, had been organized at Charleston in 1690. Blacks were no doubt connected with this church from the beginning. As early as 1817 the city records show that a burial ground of Old Circular Church had been set apart for the "use of colored people" who were members of the church. Long before the War Between the States the Congregational Church at Charleston had had at least 400 Black members.

Blacks were also found among the fellowship of the Puritan fathers in the South at the Old Midway Congregational Church in Liberty County, Georgia. The history of Old Midway dates back to the American Revolution, and at one time this church claimed 800 Afro-American members.

Except, however, for these few hundred Blacks scattered thinly in seven states in the Midwest, New England, and on the southeast coast, before 1867 Congregationalism had made no outright attempts to establish churches for and among Blacks in America. When the American Missionary Association was called to the new frontier of the South, the immediate and urgent needs

—created by slavery, war, and freedom—incumbent upon Blacks were primarily education and charitable relief. Throughout the war the ministry of the association had been structured in response to these pressing demands rather than toward the establishment of Congregational churches.

The success of the AMA in converting the Freedmen and establishing churches of the "New England faith" had not reached the expectations of some of its supporters as fully as had its advancement in the field of education. This comparative lack of success of the association in regard to establishing churches as institutions independent of the schools can be attributed in some measure to the fact that the AMA saw education as a greater need and directed most of its energy and resources to this end. On the other hand, the association was greatly bewildered because it could not fully measure the Black person's indigenous religious tradition. It was perplexed by this peculiar expression of Christianity, which was so radically unlike its own. Reflecting upon the situation as she saw it, one AMA missionary teacher remarked, in a way which has unpleasant implications for Blacks and whites as well, "The great and sorrowful fact in regard to the mass of the colored churches in the South is their want of a practical morality. They do not need more preaching or worship or enthusiasm but an entirely new ideal of Christian character."[1]

Searching, then, for a common ground through which to close the wide gap between two distinct cultural, moral, and religious traditions, and striving to lay a solid foundation upon which to establish Congregational churches and New England culture, "simple and pure," the association knew that the most logical channel through which this "illogical" and "immoral" society could be transformed was the Christian schools.[2] In spite of this duality—except for the strenuous efforts made through the school to establish a sober, moral, and intelligent faith, theocratically conceived—the AMA hesitated to venture out to start new Congregational churches as separate entities from the schools.

There had been, however, some effort made by Congregational missionaries in the independent Black churches, which had been and were being formed before, during, and after the war. But the aim here was principally "to enlighten and lift"[3] these churches to a "Congregational" understanding of the faith. The missionaries (the ordained ministers on the field) and teachers of the association labored in independent Black churches instead of gathering separate congregations and sabbath schools of their own. The ordained ministers that the AMA sent to the field "thought they could accomplish more by preaching in crowded churches under the Negro preachers [the independent Black churches] than to begin a church and to preach to the few who would come to hear."[4] Perplexed and bewildered by the Black socio-religious tradition, the association endeavored to minister in areas where it felt it could be more useful and in ways in which it was more experienced and secure. "Evangelization through education and acculturation" rather than through institutional church establishment remained its essential thrust and concern.

When the war ended in 1865, however, many more AMA supporters in the North felt strongly that the urgent need for relief and education had passed and that the association should now restrict its missionary enterprise to evangelical preaching and the establishment of churches. Those who supported this effort grew in number and strength. Among them were those who insisted that the work among Freedmen be divided. They felt that all educational work should be left to the Freedmen's Aid Societies, while the AMA should devote its total effort to "evangelical operations." Those who supported this division of labor believed that no missionary or religious organization could adequately perform the work of educating the Freedmen in the South and that the two departments of "Christian and intellectual culture [were] so distinct that they [could not] be carried forward by the same organization."[5]

In July 1866, in response to the pressures and insistence that it abandon its educational work and give priority to the "propagation of the Gospel," the American Missionary Association issued this statement:

We wish now to state briefly, that no such division of labor is contemplated:

1. Because the instruction of the people is a legitimate part of our work—the charter of the American Missionary Association making distinct provision for educational efforts;

2. Because the division would be highly inexpedient, uneconomical and injurious, and,

3. [Because] we cannot abandon our educational work among the freedmen without forfeiting more than half our power to do them good and diminishing the real benefits done to them, far more than could be compensated for by any fancied [consequences] resulting from our relinquishment of it.[6]

The association felt that as a missionary society it could not without "unfaithfulness . . . [to the Freedman] and to God relinquish to other [more secular] boards [its] . . . efforts for their education. Most especially [it] . . . could not require a Christian standing in their teachers. . . ."[7] It conceived of all phases of its ministry to the Freedmen (supplied by these boards) as "one work" that could not be divided:

The minister of Christ, the missionary of the Cross, the missionary society which would attempt to divide it and preach the gospel with no regard to the destitute's condition [as over against] their desire for education, [these functions would be] stripped of half its power and would not be welcomed by the people.[8]

The AMA was acutely aware that the strength of its immediate appeal to the Freedmen was not its sober and unfamiliar institutional expression of the faith. Rather, its appeal rested in the theocratic ideal, the power to educate and prepare the Freedmen for responsible Christian personhood and citizenship in all phases of the new, uncertain life of the free.

In a final effort to dismiss the pressures that came from those who lent hearty support but who insisted that the association "plant the church," the AMA issued this emphatic statement in 1866:

As a matter, therefore, of strict economy in pecuniary things; as seeking the best welfare of the colored people; and in faithfulness to Christ and those who seek to do his work, the AMA, while bidding others God-speed in all their labors of love in their efforts for Southern evangelization, the Association will continue to do what God in His providence evidently laid upon it.[9]

Despite this forthrightly stated position, the controversy continued and grew.

The most decisive—or perhaps threatening—pressures upon

the association, however, came from the Congregational churches and associations that had pledged to it their support in "pecuniary things." Interestingly enough, however, the *American Missionary*, after it had issued the statement of 1866, did not report having received letters or opinions from those who must certainly have been equally persistent in their demand that the association "plant the church." In May 1868, however, the veil of silence was broken and *The Congregationalist*, the monthly news organ of the Congregational churches, published an article that seemed to reverse the AMA's stance in regard to establishing churches.

The article was, in effect, a major policy statement. It indicated that the National Council of Congregational Churches, in commending the association as the organ through which the Freedmen might be reached, expected that in connection with the work of education and physical relief the AMA would proceed as rapidly as possible to establish churches of the Congregational polity and faith. The statement further indicated that "the obstacles in the way of [establishing churches] . . . [could] hardly be comprehended by those [unfamiliar] with the work."[10] One such obstacle to which the statement alluded was the "fact that Congregationalism was a name unknown and unheard of among the Blacks. The other denominations had spread Southward, but Congregationalism, by its very instinct of liberty and equality had stopped short of the Mason and Dixon's line."[11]

The writer of the article reasoned that the association had needed time to show Blacks that Congregationalism was not "some monster that might devour the churches for which they had a peculiar jealousy. And especially was time needed to educate a generation who could intelligently receive [Congregational] polity."[12] With notable conviction, the author of the statement continues:

> It took four or five years to accomplish these results. But, at last, the blacks see that those who have labored with them so long and so unselfishly cannot be bad people. They are learning too, that of all the denominations, Congregationalism, alone, never owned, nor sold a slave. This is beginning to tell, especially on those who have received, to some extent, the culture of the schools, and they are turning away from their ignorant

preachers, and demanding something more rational, and quiet, than they find in their churches.

In view of facts like these, it seems to us clear, that the time to propagate the faith of our Fathers in the Southern field has fully come, and that the New England Church is, henceforward, to keep company with the New England School.

The new policy of the American Missionary Association, then, was to establish churches with a diligence equal to that with which it had established schools. Having registered this new direction, however, the writer then reveals that Black churches of the Congregational polity and faith were already being organized in five southern states. The organization of churches was already in progress at Charleston, South Carolina; Atlanta, Georgia; Chattanooga, Nashville, and Memphis, Tennessee; Talladega, Alabama; Macon, Georgia; Camp Nelson and Berea, Kentucky; and Selma, Alabama. All these newly organized churches were comparatively small; the largest claimed about 225 members.

The relative smallness of these churches was attributed to the fact that in the words of one writer most of them were no more than a year old and that it was

the settled policy of the Association to begin at the foundation, and to admit members only on careful examination, so using all reasonable security for their purity. The old churches are full of ignorance and superstition, and wildfire, and vice, and it is found practically impossible to secure an intelligent, devoted, and virtuous membership except by beginning *de novo* in the way we have moved. The result, so far, has been that those who come from the old churches are of a better sort, while those who join on profession are largely young men and women taught, and converted in our schools. It will become apparent to anyone that churches, thus formed, with a reasonable time to grow, will become a controlling power in a dark land.[13]

Those who read this article in the May 1868 edition of *The Congregationalist* were well pleased at having learned of the association's "experimentation" in founding Black Congregational churches in the South.

By December 1869 eleven additional churches were established, making a total of twenty-one. These were "houses of worship of an aggregate valuation of $50,000. . . . With possibly few exceptions, . . . [these churches were] composed of members who on the score of intelligence and piety, would [have found] admission to any of the churches in the North."[14]

Although the "new" ministry of the association met with relative success to the extent that by 1871 there were 45 Congregational churches for Blacks in the South under its care (only 3 of these churches were connected with association schools), it always pursued its task with caution and realistic concern. In a survey of the association's work in starting new churches, Field-Secretary Smith, in the annual report of 1870, analyzed the difficulties of and promises for future growth. In reaction to the highly emotional and non-Western character of the Afro-American socio-religious tradition, Smith felt that the Congregational churches should serve as models for the independent Black churches and denominations in their respective communities. The new churches of the Pilgrim fathers were to be "cities set upon a hill." They were to "inculcate and encourage order and propriety, and an intelligent form of worship"[15] in the neighboring churches. Through this witness of the Congregational churches among Blacks in the South, it was believed that the independent Black churches would soon come to realize that "their own wild and heathenish forms of worship" were unsatisfactory and they would eventually be "transformed."[16] This transformation, Smith quite simplistically believed, could best be "accomplished by placing an orderly Christian church along side of theirs." But the greatest impact of these young Congregational churches, he felt, would be rendered by the Black members of these churches who were and would continually be "trained to be Christian in their lives." As these sober, moral, and regenerate Congregationalists moved in their communities, they would be an example and "divine revelation" for many Christians of the Black church tradition. In these Congregationalists, unmistakably members of the covenant community of the redeemed, the whole community could see that "conversion implies a different life, as well as a profession," a moral and theocratic responsibility as well as emotional assent.[17]

But Secretary Smith sensed another difficulty in establishing churches of the New England culture and faith that could be neither easily avoided nor overcome. This opposing strength was not denominational loyalty or competing sectarian interest but the Black religious and social tradition. As we noted earlier, this tradition had long been entrenched and was contradictory to the standard and theocratic conceptions of the American Missionary Association. Smith wrote, therefore:

I used to attribute the indifference of the colored people and the opposition of the ministers of these churches to a sectarian feeling, from the fact that they were neither distinctly Methodist nor Baptist—the prevailing denominations. There was something in this, but I am satisfied that our difficulty has been in the fact that we have tried to establish a moral and intelligent Christianity! And I am confirmed in this by the fact that whenever our Baptist brethren have tried to establish a church on the same basis, discarding the ignorant preacher and disallowing excesses, they have met with the same indifference and opposition from their colored Baptist brethren; and I am sure that they will learn before long, if they have not already made the discovery, that their hope as a denomination in the South is with the young, trained in churches planted and controlled by men of their own appointment.

It is in preparation for such churches that half the colored children in all our schools have been under tuition these five years past; and for the Baptist leaders in the North to caution their churches to "beware of the American Missionary Association" is just as wise as for the master of a becalmed ship to call upon his crew to beware of a breeze that begins to fill his sails!

These facts respecting existing churches in the South have an important bearing on all questions connected with the future of the colored people. Their friends in the North ought to know that when they help a colored church they are not necessarily doing anything to help the race, and may be doing the opposite. For these churches, so thoroughly entrenched in absurdity, ignorance, and immorality, will be strongholds of resistance to good influences, when other barriers are given way. The greatest opposition now to our school comes from the ignorant preachers of these churches. They understand that an educated generation will make an end to their occupation, and they do what they can, without arousing the indignation of their flock, in many ways, to thwart the teachers and cripple the schools.[18]

Fully aware of the difficulties and opposing intensity presented by the socio-religious tradition that it proposed to transform and redeem, Congregationalism nonetheless stubbornly had with dedication accepted the challenge to plant and to be the church, to establish the theocracy of the New England culture and way, and to become "a controlling power in a dark land."

Chapter 7
"Indulging a Christian Hope"

The reduction of life on the border to the bare funda-
mentals of physical and social existence, the dearth of
intellectual stimulation and the lack of those effective
inhibitions of emotional expression which formal education cultivates, the awesome manifestations of nature,
the effects of which were not checked by the sense of
safely permanent dwellings and the nearness of other
men convey, all these made the settler subject to the
feverish phenomena of revivalism.

—H. Richard Niebuhr
The Social Sources of Denominationalism

Augustus Field Beard, a former general secretary of the American Missionary Association, calls the decade beginning in 1875
"The Decade of Concentration." It was during this period that
the association increased its efforts to initiate Congregational
churches among Blacks in the South. Because of the immensity
of its responsibility in the homeland, the AMA withdrew from all
its foreign work with one exception—the Mendi Mission in Sierra
Leone, West Africa. The association envisioned these two fields
as part of one work. Blacks trained in AMA churches and schools
could be used for the Christianization and transformation of their
brothers and sisters in Africa. "The pleadings for . . . [Congrega-
tional churches among Blacks in the South] were constant, and
there were many tentative experiments to meet these requests."[1]

The association was led to fulfill these requests and to respond
to the challenge of the new frontier because of the image it had of
itself, given in the "church-forming" revelation of the early
Christian *ecclesia* and the church of the Puritan fathers. As is

true, however, of all human institutions and endeavors, there were mixed motivations entertained by many supporters of the association. Those who supported it were also concerned with preserving the broad base of the "American"—and particularly the New England-Puritan—tradition, which it conceived in Congregational and Anglo-Saxon Protestant terms.

To be sure, "domestication" or "taming" of the Freedmen was an overwhelming concern of many contributors to the AMA program. Many felt that the religion and culture of New England could be effectively used to stem the tide of the Black "threat of violence" against the white community in America. This religion and culture could also protect the Freedmen against southern political bigotry and control. Such attitudes were greatly reminiscent of those of the white southern church constituency toward the Afro-American "brother in the Lord" prior to the war. Nonetheless, the Congregational churches, quite independently picking up from the southern white pattern, flirted with lesser motives as well. The most representative statement of this political and social position was recorded in the *American Missionary* as early as July 1863 and was echoed in varying degrees through the early decades of the twentieth century in many issues that followed. Consistent with this "unpure" motivation in the Black South, one person wrote:

> I feel deeply that our churches must arise and shake themselves as from the dust, and meet the mighty avalanche of emancipated mind in this country, and Christianize it or be crushed by it. The plantation system of whips and fetters and dark ignorance, and bitter, mindless and motiveless toil, has imbruted the bondsmen, and when the terrible pressure of that system is taken off, nothing but the grace of God, through the motives of Christianity, can keep the Freedmen from accepting their own brutal and base passions as their masters, in place of those whom they have left. The problem of our national salvation is to be wrought out upon their minds, after war and battle are done; and we have not a moment to lose. If the demagogues of the country, who have resisted their freedom, will be the first to use them when free, and, by using make them ever more corrupt and dark-minded than they are now.[2]

Aside from the fear of Black corruption, aggression, and defiance, guilt was another factor in motivating Congregational ministry among Blacks in the South. Another writer says:

> We must never forget that the Lord God is Governor among nations; that he governs them by fixed laws, and that neither this nation nor any other can escape his retributive justice. As a nation we have sinned and provoked the God of heaven and earth. To say nothing of other transgressions at this time, slavery has been the country's sin. It is true that the seat of slavery has been chiefly at the South, but the people of the North have consented to the deed; and therefore the sin is national.[3]

An example of guilt as a factor (on a more personal basis) among other motives is evidenced in this material:

> Enclosed is a draft for one hundred dollars from _____, for the Freedmen, a donation to the American Missionary Association. This, perhaps, may be called conscience-money. [The donor] feels a little troubled that he has so long used cotton that was a product of slave-labor, and now is willing to make up as fast as he can to the poor Freedmen, for the sin of using cotton polluted with the blood and sweat of slavery. This suggestion may stir up the pure minds of others, whose consciences may be stirred in the same direction. If so, we hope that your treasury may overflow with abundance to supply the great demand for men and money for the Freedmen.[4]

It becomes apparent, then, that many Congregationalists knew that slavery had been the "nation's sin." Now that the war was over, both the North and the South must share the burden of guilt and responsibility that emancipation brought. It would thus appear that ministry among the Freedmen for personal, religious, and political reasons as well as the expiation of sin and guilt were two significant factors that stimulated the concern and effort to establish the Congregational spirit and churches among Blacks in the South.

The effort to establish churches on the new frontier was also given impetus by Roman Catholic missionary activity, which represented a formidable threat to any theocratic illusions Congregationalism might have entertained. Between 1861 and 1890,

10,373,628 immigrants entered the United States. A large percentage of these immigrants were Roman Catholics. The efforts of the Roman Catholics to win the allegiance of the Freedmen were indeed "avowed and energetic."

> The avowal [to proselytize Freedmen] was made in the Romish Council held in Baltimore in 1866, and the energy of the effort (was) . . . attested by the millions of dollars then voted; by the collections taken in Catholic churches; by the many priests employed in the South; by the education of 100 colored young men at Rome, most of them designated for [the southern Black] . . . field; and by extensive educational efforts in the South, not only in common schools, but by schools of so high an order as to attract many of the most talented colored youth![5]

Besides these "threatening" efforts of the Church of Rome to convert Blacks of the South, it was believed that Catholicism inherently possessed emotive and "liturgical" appeals that might have a "strong hold" on the "colored race." In the first place, the AMA felt that the Catholics were equipped to appeal to the Freedmen's "love of display." It was believed that many Blacks would be attracted by the "gaudy trappings and gorgeous ceremonies and [that] the Catholic vestments and services [would] offer these in fascinating frequency and splendor."[6] The colorful, ethereal mystery of Roman Catholic "Medieval Pageantry," it was held, might well have strong attraction for untutored minds open to wonder, mystery, awe.

Second, the American Missionary Association was aware that in comparison with American Protestantism, particularly in the southern and border states, the Church of Rome had a "broad basis on which it [placed] . . . all the sons of Adam and the Redeemed of Christ. In the cathedral and church it [ranked] . . . all worshippers alike, the richest and the poorest—the men of all colors and climes—[knelt] . . . together around a common altar and . . . [worshiped] a common Father."[7] The association feared that "thinking men of color" would be "constrained to say: 'This, so far, is God's religion.' "[8]

Acknowledging the preeminent power and appeal of the Roman Catholic Church, the association prophetically announced in 1875:

The Protestant Church has yet much to do in overcoming her exclusiveness, and in helping to educate the colored people before it can vindicate itself before the law of its own conscience or the just demands of the Negro race. . . . Protestants who will not believe that the Catholics are making efforts among the Freedmen, and who are so indifferent in regard to the fate of these ex-slaves, may wake up ere long to discover that things have gone too far to be remedied—that Rome has got the vantage ground and that her victory is sure. When the day dawns, that gives Rome the control over the votes of the millions of these ex-slaves, then Papal supremacy in America is assured.[9]

From this point in time we know that it was the evil of white supremacy and disfranchisement of the Negro (rather than papal authority and Roman political control) that was more greatly to be feared and exposed. Despite these realities, the association, motivated by fear, guilt, and the menacing power of the Church of Rome, and driven still by a sense of responsible vocation and the theocratic ideal, felt more urgently than ever the need to be and plant the churches of the Congregational variety.

Beginning in the "Decade of Concentration" through the remainder of the nineteenth century, the American Missionary Association constantly sought ways by which Congregational churches among Afro-Americans in the South could be expediently but wisely established and maintained. Although the school remained an essential instrument of the church, other channels had to be discovered and experimented with if the new churches among the ex-slaves were to survive and increase.

The first significant channel by which the association sought to extend Congregational churches among Blacks in the South was the revival, the "Precious Ingathering." The missionaries and ministers of the AMA were soon aware that the socio-religious ethos of the Freedmen was filled with a seething emotionalism that could not be contained. As we noted earlier, this fervor was a part of the Black church tradition that had to be considered and in some ways used if Congregationalism was to strike a familiar, harmonious, and meaningful chord among Black people, and if the young churches were to multiply and grow. "The Negros, like [all] the disinherited, required an emotional, empirical religion.

'The heart depressed by drudgery, hardship, forlornness craves not merely moral guidance but exhilaration and ecstasy.' ''[10] The association was challenged to respond to this craving and need.

The American Missionary Association came into the South at a time when revivalism swept through and claimed the entirety of Black life. No one dared to predict the how, where, and when of the "visitation" and "indwelling" of the "Spirit of the Lord." The joy of being free, the bewilderment and frustrations of a totally new pattern of life, and the search for a fixed and certain center around which one could integrate the inner self and find oneness with the "world soul" and meaning in a confused and hostile world left the Negro with the ambiguous feeling that the "Lord was hidden but near"—that the "Precious Master Jesus" was "teasing" his way into the history and life of Dixie and would "show them who he was." But only in a dramatic, emotional conversion would this charismatic breakthrough occur, and then the Spirit would appear and change the painful course of events of Black history and life.

Edward Bull, an AMA teacher and preacher in Beaufort, North Carolina in 1870, reports an incident that occurred in the Beaufort school that illumines the extent to which the whole Black ethos was filled with emotion and the "Holy Ghost" and subject to break into exaltation at any place and time:

> Yesterday morning when we opened the school—after a week's vacation—the religious feeling was too deep to permit the scholars to pursue their studies. All seemed desirous to seek and secure the salvation of their souls. And when one of the scholars came in who had just begun to rejoice in a new-found Savior, and by some motion or expression, showed her joy and happiness, their feelings were deeply stirred, and they broke out into weeping, and sobbing and praying. The regular exercises of the school had to be set aside, and the teachers passed around among them speaking such words of counsel and comfort as they were able. The neighbors and parents came into the number fifteen or twenty, and looked on in wonder and amazement. Indeed nothing prevented the breaking up into a noisy, demonstrative "meeting," but the strict discipline of the school. At

length they were dismissed in regular order, the scholars passing out one by one. Today it is more quiet, but the religious feeling is too deep to allow of much study. About a dozen of our scholars are indulging a Christian hope.[11]

Even in this "holy" emotional history, the stern sobriety of the Congregational tradition would not allow full assent to an emotive religious expression. But the association realized that the revival was a logical and, indeed, a necessary expression, and must be cautiously used:

A merely emotional piety is one of the dangers of the colored people. The great aim of their religious culture should be to develop principle and morality. But we must not go too far in repressing their emotions. While the feelings are not all of religion, there is no full-ordered religion without them. The defect of the piety of the white race is that it has too little emotion. . . . Indeed our Methodist brethren have fairly monopolized the most of this emotional piety. And herein, we are persuaded, lies one of the main secrets of their power over the masses; for the soul craves this exercise of the emotional nature; its wants cannot be met with mere forms, properties or activities.

One of the most beautiful and blessed effects of a real Christian culture for the Negro will be the reflex influence of his emotive religion upon the unimaginative and unemotional white people who are now benefiting him.[12]

As an outgrowth of the combined feeling of suspicious contempt and appreciative wonder for the fervent response to the gospel of the Black religious tradition, as early as the last half of the year 1868 there is decisive indication that revivals had begun and would increase in the Congregational churches and schools. "Inquirers' groups" were formed with success; numerous conversions were witnessed; "prayer and praise" meetings sprang into Congregational life and were well attended by the religious enthusiasts among the Freedmen.

The Congregational revivals, however, were "marked by quietude, deep conviction of sin, and clear evidence of acceptance"[13] and regeneration. Although deep religious feelings prevailed at these "precious ingatherings," the expression of these feelings was not identical with that of the more typical Black faiths. For example, the Rev. John Scott (founder and minister of the church at Dudley, North Carolina, the first Black Congregational church in that state) describes the simplicity and dignity of the revival that took place there:

> We are experiencing the most remarkable and the most powerful revival of religion that I have ever witnessed among these people. It has given me new confidence in God and the Freedmen. Most of the revivals here are scenes of great religious excitement, but our meetings have been still, without response or motion. Last Sabbath night while we were speaking, one head after another bowed, and soon the silent tear gave way to an audible but suppressed sob, which soon became general, and we were a weeping audience; thinking of the love of Christ, thinking of the value of a soul. . . . The ability of the colored [people] to reason calmly and to perceive clearly the force of religious truth is in this revival clearly established as well as the pressing need of an intelligent Christian ministry, instead of a wild, ignorant class, to lead this people.[14]

The quiet, calm revivals and precious ingatherings continued in the churches well into the twentieth century. Beginning in 1885 and as late as 1916, a full-time evangelist from England, the Rev. James Wharton, was under the employ of the AMA. The Congregational missionaries and ministers, unaccustomed as they were to emotional or "revivalistic" display, continued to suppress the Black church tradition and to replace it with the more culturally desirable New England faith.

It was no accident that the revivals were generally more prevalent where the AMA had provided schools.[15] Here the situation was more controlled. An intellectual, sober base had been laid, the desired "Congregational end" could be obtained. In the twentieth century the revivals became more and more "New England-ized" and subdued. Eventually the revivals became simply a program series or season of the church year. The revival pattern, after many years of use, lost its spontaneity and became a sterile ritual, a liturgical form. It was at this point that the revivals proved powerless to summon to repentance people who were acquainted with and in need of a more fervent "call."

Perhaps a more significant factor in the growth and increase of Congregationalism among Blacks in the South during the nineteenth and early twentieth centuries was the establishment of a theological curriculum in the AMA colleges. These theological programs, of course, were established to equip "able young men" for a ministry in the churches. The Black church tradition, it may be recalled, placed little emphasis on an educated ministry. To some extent this was due to the fact that there had been no schools in which the clergy could be trained. But, more significantly, this deficient emphasis upon the training of clergy in the Black church can be attributed to the belief that "if God 'called' . . . [a person he or she] needed little or no academic preparation. God would see to it that the 'anointed one' was in every respect equipped for [the] task."[16] Of equal significance, perhaps, was the fact that "there were urgent church needs to be met"[17] and people had no time to waste in the schools. In contrast to the position of many of the Black church tradition in regard to a trained clergy, the New England Congregationalists—who could and would not be easily persuaded to separate learning and faith —were convinced that the strength and integrity of the Black churches could and must be lifted by an educated clergy trained in theological schools.

As early as 1869 there is indication that there was an embryo school of divinity at the institution which later became known as Talladega College at Talladega, Alabama. The Rev. Henry E. Brown, the school's first principal, was the master and instructor of the theological course.[18] In that year the association reports that Brown was "preparing to send out several students every Saturday to fill regular appointments on the Sabbath within a circuit of 10 miles."[19] Under his able leadership as many as twenty students, just four years out of slavery, were brought together at Talladega College for theological training as candidates for the Congregational ministry or (according to their own preference) for the ministry of the church of the Afro-American variety and tradition.

By 1871 plans were being laid at Talladega College, Fisk University, Tougaloo College, Howard University, Straight University (now Dillard University), and at Atlanta University to raise the level of the theological curricula and to organize seminaries as distinct departments of the schools. These departments were to replace the old "come as you are and stay as long as you can" theological course and were commended to "all who desire(d) to see the Faith of the Pilgrim Fathers prevail in the South."[20]

Aside from the "marked and salutory" influence the new theological departments were to have upon the churches in their respective regions, the AMA seminaries would also meet the educational needs of ministers of other denominations that had few Black schools of divinity of their own.[21] Owing to the importunity of poverty and age, most of the students were compelled to pursue the theological curriculum in connection with their normal or college course. Some became full-time preachers before their training was complete.

In general, the theological curriculum of the schools had three basic emphases, all of which were related to "practical" Christian service:

(1) to make pupils familiar with the facts of the Bible;
(2) to establish them in a system of Christian theology;
(3) to acquaint them with the best methods of Christian work.[22]

The association and the Congregational churches, especially those near the seminaries, were greatly encouraged by the possibilities and contributions toward denominational expansion afforded by the theological schools. When the Central South Conference (embracing all AMA schools and churches in Tennessee, Georgia, Alabama, and Mississippi) met in Selma, Alabama, November 10-12, 1874, several students from the theological department of Atlanta University were examined for candidacy to the Christian ministry, in which event the conference, deeply encouraged and greatly pleased,

> resolved, that we have participated with great satisfaction in the examination of the students from Atlanta University, as candidates for the Christian Ministry, and we congratulate the Churches upon this event, occurring for the first time in the history of the Conference, which gives us assurance that we may hope for a regular and frequent addition to the ranks of the ministry from the young men now being educated in our institutions.[23]

The limited and fragmentary nature of the data concerning the precise relationship of the seminaries to the establishment and maintenance of the churches does not lend itself to statistical analysis. The very fact, however, that so many of the churches were clustered about the schools in almost concentric patterns, and the fact that the churches served as training centers for the students, would certainly imply that the seminaries were greatly responsible for many of the churches' creation and growth. It is significant that when the Alabama association met on April 3, 1888, eleven of the fourteen delegates present were from churches ministered by students or graduates of the Talladega College Seminary. Since there were only seventeen churches in the association, this eleven represented better than 65 percent.

Significant relationships between the establishment and strength of churches and their closeness to the theological departments could also be recounted. Yet the greater significance of the schools consisted in the contribution they made in the perpetuation of New England culture and the Congregational idea. The churches pastored by the graduates of the association's theological schools were described as

> centers of life, around which the moral and social elements . . . organized themselves in order and beauty. They [were said to] set the standard for other churches. They . . . married morality to religion . . . inculcated temperance . . . encouraged economy and industry, so that many of their members became home owners; softened or removed prejudices and commanded the respect of the best white people, and demonstrated the capacity of the race for the best of civilization.[24]

The influence of the southern Black Congregational churches in the late nineteenth century cannot be measured arithmetically. This influence must be measured in terms of the parable of the leaven. The association knew that if it stood by the Puritan principle its progress denominationally would be slow.[25] On rare occasions, however, its enthusiasm for the success and vitality of the work led it to ponder policies and procedures that were alien to the Congregational idea. Among such alien policies that the AMA discussed were the appointment of a "bishop" for the southern Black field and the formulation of a "Congregational Freedmen's

Creed." It was proposed that this bishop be located at some central station and that the bishop establish churches when and where they were needed, visit them quarterly, impose the ordinances of the church, and seek and appoint any who were qualified to "exhort."[26]

The proposal for the formulation of a creed for the Freedmen came from the Central South Conference meeting at Memphis, Tennessee in 1881. It was proposed that this creed be suited to the "average intelligence" of the Freedmen who "applied for admission" to the churches with the hope that it would facilitate an increase in membership of the Black Congregational churches in the South. The conference believed that

> these children of nature, with their ready faith but crude culture, coming into the inheritance and this New Testament way of the churches, need the "sincere milk of the Word"—a declaration of doctrine that shall not be in the nomenclature nor philosophy of a past, but in the language and after the spirit of our approved New England theology. They need a form of sound words such as that when they have once learned it they will not need to be taught over again of its phraseology.[27]

The quest for "success" brought with it many temptations to temper the Congregational idea. But the polity and integrity of the Puritan faith and tradition would not entertain alien procedures and strange appeals. Needless to say, the association and the Congregational National Council never appointed a "bishop" and never formulated a "Freedmen's Creed." The nineteenth-century advancement of the Congregational churches, as compared with the independent churches of the Black religious tradition, therefore remained decidedly slow.[28]

At the annual meeting of the AMA in Cleveland, Ohio, in 1882, the Committee on Church Work reported that the rate of progress since 1865 had been uniformly constant, with a near average of five churches established each year. In the four-year period between 1882 and 1887, forty-four churches were organized. This was better than double the annual organization rate for the previous seventeen years. The average membership of these churches was sixty-two communicants per congregation. Although the rate of increase was relatively small when compared with the growth of the independent Black churches during the same period, it was a large and encouraging figure when compared with an average of only forty-three members per Congregational church on the frontier west of the Mississippi River. The available statistics for church expansion and development for the late years of the nineteenth century are confusing, to say the least. Black and white churches were not recorded separately, and some of the impressive figures (e.g., church membership) may represent some margins of error in their calculations. It seems safe to say from the available data, however, that increase was constantly counterbalanced by decline. Many churches were dropped as changing or unstable conditions of communities made it impossible or unwise to continue them. Others were closed by default or defeat, while still others defected to the independent kinship of the Black religious fold.

Despite the struggles, failures, and defeats witnessed during the nineteenth century, the American Missionary Association seemed constantly driven by the call to transform and by the vision it had of itself as God's colony in the human world. Determined by an arrogant assumption and weakness that was its earthly integrity and strength, the association knew that that help which comes by way of influence and not authority was most consistent with the church-forming genius of the Puritan ancestors. This genius of spirit confesses that all people are children of God, yet recognizes the duty of age, culture, and tradition to share what they believe to be their "good" things with those whose history has prohibited aspirations toward an essentially different cultural and religious ideal.

Chapter 8
"That the Circumference of These Span"

Numerically speaking organized Negro Congregationalism in the South is not a large thing. The churches number only about 150 with about 10,000 members. The
work of the Association among them is represented by
83 ministers who serve in about 140 churches and by a
fraternal and advisory relation to the whole group.

Two-thirds of the churches are in the 3 states of Alabama, Georgia and North Carolina in which the large
part of the school work of the Association has been
located. They are essentially the children of the schools,
either located in the same communities, or in the city
centers where graduates of the schools form colonies.

The rural churches as a group suffer more from ignorance, extreme poverty and often fluctuating populations. Yet nowhere can one find more satisfaction than
in some of the better country churches among the home-
owning communities.

American Missionary Association,
66th Annual Report, 1911-12

As indicated in Chapter 2, Congregationalists have always had
a strong sense of having been set apart as chosen people in the
process of world redemption. They have indulged the hope that
the regenerate peoples who are brought into and who participate
in the Congregational covenant community will show evidence of
having been redeemed through an appropriate and transforming
witness as citizens of God's colony in the human world.

As the dawn of the twentieth century broke upon the life and work of the American Missionary Association, the AMA harkened to the challenge of a new day. It knew that to transform Black religion and culture with integrity and vigor it must draw unto itself those who would become leaders. In a sense, this had been the association's understanding of its task from the beginning, and the purpose for which it established the schools. With the mission of planting churches before it, it was now of paramount importance that this ideal not be obscured.

Congregationalism among Blacks in the South was destined from its beginning to become a movement for the social and intellectual elite. How could it become otherwise when the demands that its dynamic tradition placed on it were so great and the integrity and quality of its leaders were so exacting? Congregationalism, with no creeds to propound and with no sectarian axes to grind, could give of itself with unmatched freedom and love, but always and only with a fixed image of what the church and society should be. This image was an outgrowth of its experience in the New England Puritan Way. Constantly in search of leaders and noble people among the ex-slaves, the association determined to lay claim upon the Black elite.

To the surprise of many, the bourgeois class of Afro-Americans antedated the Emancipation Proclamation and formed a conspicuous core in the Black community in the years immediately after the Civil War. In his book *Black Bourgeoisie*, E. Franklin Frazier describes the rise of this particular group in the Black community:

> At the end of the 19th century and the beginning of the 20th century, a class structure slowly emerged [in the Black community in America, especially in the cities and towns] which was based upon social distinctions such as education and conventional behavior rather than on occupation and income. At the top of the pyramid was a small upper class. The superior status of this class was due chiefly to its differentiation from the great mass of the Negro population because of mixed ancestry. The family heritage consisted of traditions of civilized behavior and economic efficiency. The members' light skin color was indicative not only of their white ancestry but of their descent from Negroes who were free before the

Civil War, or who had enjoyed the advantages of having lived in the houses of their masters. This class constantly incorporated those Negroes who were able to acquire an education in the schools supported by Northern philanthropy.[1]

The AMA churches connected with the schools were in an enviable position to attract and possess the leaders among the Black social elite. In 1912, Secretary Augustus Field Beard observed that "what was especially marked when our schools began was the proportion of pupils who were far more Anglo-Saxon in their parentage than they were Africans."[2]

By and large, mulattoes and other Blacks who were free before the signing of the Emancipation Proclamation were among the first brought into the Congregational fold. As few and deprived as these people were, in their opportunities as well as in their intellectual and cultural level, they were far above those who were compelled to suffer the misfortunes of slavery through the end of the war. The association saw potential leaders among this privileged class and brought them into the churches and schools.

A case in point is the Avery Institute in Charleston, South Carolina. Here privileged Blacks, many of them mulattoes, were in the majority and among the first to affiliate with this AMA school. Struck by this phenomenon at Avery, the *Charleston Daily News* carried an article in May 1866 describing the class pattern and social constituency of the school:

> One-fourth of the pupils were born free and these comprise the more advanced classes. The school, therefore, must not be considered a fair average of colored education in the city. As it is the design to make this a school for the education of the teachers, the best material has been retained as far as practicable and the remainder sent to other schools. Thus in some classes scarcely a pure black is seen. The greater number in the more advanced classes are very fair; but all lines are represented. All were very neat and well dressed, and bore themselves with credit to themselves and to their teachers.[3]

Not only was there an inevitable class stratification in the AMA schools, in greater or lesser degree, but the upper echelon of the

Black community (in part because of the fact that many members of the churches had been trained and steeped in the cultural tradition of the schools) was highly represented in many of the AMA churches as well. For example, before 1900 a minister of one of the churches in Alabama wrote:

> Most of our members own their own homes and some of them are as tastefully arranged and furnished as most homes among the better class whites. In the getting of homes our folk, as a rule, set the example for the rest of the community. They are usually the first to own their own homes and not a few of these homes are models of neatness and refinement. . . . That young doctor spoke rightly the other night when he said to me, "your church is bound to be the coming church among the better class of the colored people. Where intelligence and morality are encouraged, there intelligence, refinement and morality are bound to go."[4]

It should be noted, perhaps with dismay, that the association never maintained that it was against a system of class, nor would it, in fact, clearly recognize that it was more disposed to the social elite which it came to depend upon to advance the kingdom of the New England Congregational Way. Indeed, it was opposed not to class and social distinctions but rather to caste, and it insisted that there was an "ethical" distinction between class and caste discrimination. As a member of a particular caste, one is locked into a given level of privilege—or nonprivilege—as over against patterns of class that allow for upward mobility on the basis of merit.

The AMA stood firm against caste on the basis that "it excludes people from common rights and privileges. It degrades people on the grounds of race or color."[5] It believed that caste was "seen in its worst form when it appears in religious bodies."[6] In the opinion of the AMA, caste should be set aside because it had no place in the Congregational pattern and faith. On the other hand, the association believed equally firmly that class distinctions were necessary and should be maintained. Class rested, as the AMA understood it, on a different principle. It was grounded in "companionship," indeed, "sympathetic" or selective "companionship" that "has its own qualifications."[7] The AMA felt that it had "no mission to prevent the existence of classes in society. . . . "[8] It believed further that even "Christ who linked his life to the lowly, had his sympathetic [selective] companionships, but the spirit of caste was never his."[9] To do the job before it, the association selected its "companions" with extreme care. Opposed to caste but dependent upon an enlightened, responsible regenerate class, the churches became strongholds of the rising Black bourgeoisie. Strongly influenced by the persuasion that the future of Blacks in America rested upon the leadership of a creative minority composed of the intellectual elite, the AMA became almost exclusively concerned with the welfare of those churches wherein these potential leaders might be gathered.

This tendency on the part of the AMA was not without dynamic relationship to the whole demographic movement of Blacks during this period. One cannot properly overestimate the influences arising out of the urbanization of Blacks, with its consequent proliferation of educational opportunities as a vital factor in determining for the association where the locus of its efforts should hereafter be concentrated.

The first two decades of the twentieth century brought many changes in Afro-American life. Tremendous advances were made. Progress was rapid and constant, particularly for the rising elite. The increase in educational opportunities for Blacks was encouraging. Whereas it is estimated that only twenty of the 4,500,000 Blacks in the United States had received a college diploma before the Civil War, by 1910, when the Afro-American population had increased to nearly eight million, 3,856 Blacks had been graduated from American colleges with a baccalaureate degree.[10]

Aside from the continued efforts of the American Missionary Association and other missionary societies, northern philanthropy with special interest in education was an important element in improving educational conditions among the increasingly urbanized Blacks, north and south. The Slater Fund, established in 1882, and the General Education Board, the Anna T. Jeanes Fund, the Rosenwald Fund, and the Phelp-Stokes Fund (all founded after 1900) made valuable contributions to Negro and southern education.[11] As a result of these efforts, the illiteracy of

77

the Negro population ten years of age and over had decreased from 57.1 percent in 1890 to 30.4 percent in 1910.[12]

The advancement in education brought with it a relative affluence among the Black population at large. The majority of Blacks when emancipated were penniless, naked, landless, unschooled laborers. Nearly 95 percent of them were field hands and unskilled laborers of the lowest class. But by 1909 this figure had declined by at least 20 to 30 percent.[13] By 1923 it was reported that the property held by Blacks was increasing in value at the rate of 50 million dollars a year and that the property accumulation had increased in value from about 20 million dollars in 1866 to over 1.5 billion dollars through that year. It was also estimated that the 22 million acres which Blacks owned constituted a greater area than the five New England states of New Hampshire, Vermont, Massachusetts, Connecticut, and Rhode Island.[14]

Simultaneously with the increase of Black education, which brought about a relative affluence within the Black population, another significant change had taken place in Afro-American life. We have already noted that the Black population, which had always been a predominantly rural, agrarian class, gradually began to turn away from the soil toward the industrial and cultural opportunities of the cities. The urbanization trend was largely aggravated by the collapse of the one-crop system in the South; the fluctuating population, which was due to transient industries and community disruptions; and the protection and relative security from racial brutality that the numbers of the city afforded. As John Hope Franklin points out, however, the rise of the Black community in the city "was also coincident with the rise of the city in American life."[15] In 1900 there were 73 cities with more than 5,000 Negroes. Washington had more than 86,000, Baltimore 79,000, and New Orleans 77,000; Philadelphia, New York, and Memphis each had more than 50,000. The Negro population of these cities was growing rapidly. Negroes outnumbered whites in Charleston, Savannah, Montgomery, Jacksonville, Shreveport, Baton Rouge, and several other southern cities. If cities afforded larger opportunities, Negroes hoped to benefit from them.[16]

Mays and Nicholson found that "the drift of the Negro population from rural to urban centers from 1900 to 1920 caused the

Negro city population to increase 1,557,465, while that of the rural areas increased only 71,572."[17] Though some of the Black migration was absorbed by the larger urban centers in the North, there were still 162,832 more Negroes in the South in 1920 than in 1910, and the population of the southern cities witnessed a continual increase.[18]

The American Missionary Association observed these dramatic changes taking place in twentieth-century Black life with mixed emotions. On the one hand, it was disheartened because it knew that the increased mobility of the Black population would drain many of the more able Blacks from the rural communities and small towns and would necessitate the abandonment of its ministry in many of the churches on these vanishing frontiers. On the other hand, the association was encouraged. It saw in the urbanization trend a God-given possibility and advantage. In the larger southern cities Black leadership could easily be found and developed. The AMA responded to the awareness that concentration of its activity and support of the churches located in the relatively stable urban centers presented an ideal challenge and a less obvious risk.

The initial realization of the rapid educational, economic, and urban evolution which was occurring in the Black South came to the AMA in 1901 when 22 of its 122 churches were dropped as a result of fluctuations in the Black population.[19] The area that suffered the greatest loss was the turpentine-field region of Georgia. The abandonment of the work in these twenty-two churches was not due, however, to any negligence on the part of the AMA. The association desired to make this point clear.

> The excisions do not signify that the churches fell apart
> and ceased to exist while their members remained in the
> community, but that large numbers of the laboring peo-
> ple who were formerly employed and had their resi-
> dence in places where the churches were organized were
> dispersed to other localities by change of employment.[20]

As a result of increased migration from the rural areas to the urban centers and the constant fluctuations that undermined stable patterns and structures of community settlement and life, in many rural districts and small towns Blacks became greatly overchurched. Churches that were established in great numbers in years past were no longer needed to serve the more sparse populations.

Realizing these changing social patterns, in March 1915 sixty-five of the Black rural Congregational churches, at the request and under the supervision of the association, made a self-study survey of their own status and the more fundamental conditions in the communities in which they were found. The information gathered in the survey covered a total rural population of about 43,000 Blacks. Many interesting facts were unearthed. There were 212 churches, or one for every 200 and more people under survey. In the 65 communities that reported, the number of churches of all denominations ranged from two to thirteen for populations never exceeding 2,000. Six or seven churches per community were reported with great frequency, but the most frequent figures reported were three and four. The extreme cases were a community in Georgia with thirteen churches for 750 people and another in South Carolina with thirteen churches for a population of 1,000. There were only five communities with only one other Black church besides the Congregational church, with populations of 150, 250, 350, 400, and 500 persons. There was also a small town in Louisiana where the French-speaking Creoles were Roman Catholic and the only other Black church was Congregational.

Of these 65 rural Congregational churches under survey in 1915, the largest had 199 members, followed by a very few with from 100 to 120 communicants. The average church, however, had no more than 50 members on its rolls, and in the out-stations surrounding the cities or seminaries, which were more or less "sub-mission" fields, many churches claimed fewer than 20 members. In only one instance was a rural Congregational church the largest in the community.

Despite the aid the AMA had given, the church buildings and facilities were not above the general average of other Black churches, and few college or seminary graduates were in Congregational pulpits in rural communities. Most of these churches had services once a month, and almost all pastors had more than one church. Some had as many as five.

The 65 churches that responded to the survey were combined in 29 rural districts, with the exception of two or three churches yoked with city parishes. Four of the circuits received less than $100 in the fiscal year 1914 from their members. Fifteen, or better than half of the circuits, received only between $120 and $180; five collected $210 to $260, two received $300 and $350, and only one reported up to $475 for the year. It is also startling to discover that the average receipts of all the Black Congregational churches in the South during the same year were only $280. This average included any building or betterment operation that may have occurred during the year.[21]

Particularly in the rural areas, then, the Blacks were impoverished and over-churched. This the association knew. An illustrative instance of the AMA's awareness of the severe over-churching in the Black rural community can be gathered from its response to a request for the establishment of a rural Congregational church from a Black pastor in North Carolina in the year 1913. In part, the pastor enthusiastically wrote: "Three-quarters of a mile from the depot there are more than nine hundred Negroes; no white people live in the place. It has two schools, seven well built churches, paying an average salary of one hundred fifty dollars per year."[22] To the letter the editor of the *American Missionary* attached this wry note: "It is needless to report that we did not enter into this abundant opportunity for an additional Congregational Church."[23]

Even before the rural church survey of 1915 had been made regarding the means by which the association should cope with problems of increased mobility, community dislocation, urbanization, and over-churching in Black rural communities, two proposals were made. The first proposal, made in 1902, recommended the establishment of a "mobile" or "migrant" ministry that would follow parishioners wherever they settled. "A definite organization and permanent building" would be replaced by an arrangement whereby "as the people [went] elsewhere in quest of labor they [might] be followed by the preacher and his associates."[24] Since the denomination could not encompass the idea of a migrant ministry within its present plans and preferred to become an urban institutional church that served the enlightened, regenerate class, this proposal was received with little if any enthusiasm and elicited no action.

The second proposal was made by J.G. Merrill, president of

Fisk University, the AMA school in Nashville, Tennessee. Merrill entitled his proposal "Cities: The Strategic Centers of Our Missionary Work." In this essay he acknowledged the shift of population in the South from the rural to the urban centers as trends in both the Black and white communities. He reasoned that the emigration from the Black community had been precipitated by the tyranny of the Ku Klux Klan, which forced Blacks to the cities to seek the protection of a more concentrated Black population. Afro-Americans realized that lynchings were less frequent in the cities, and the tenant farmer who received far less than his due recompense for labor at harvest, discontent with subservience, had little to lose and perhaps much to gain in the urban move.

Merrill was convinced that AMA education and evangelization should be continued. He believed that the public schools and the churches of the Black religious tradition could not stem the "awful tide of ignorance, superstition and vice" that threatened the future of the entire Black community. The association should therefore continue its necessary work. On the other hand, Merrill knew that the AMA could not do both education and evangelization and should guard against the danger of spreading itself too thin. It could "only hope to succeed as it attempt[ed] to do that work which it [was] . . . equal to doing." He believed that the American Missionary Association should concentrate its church-forming and community-building efforts in the cities. He observed the major missionary, evangelistic, and educational movements that were "successful" in the nation at the beginning of the century and noted that all were located in major cities. It appeared that all major social patterns in America were directly or indirectly related to the urbanization trend. Thus, Merrill insisted that this dynamic pattern of American life should be effectively used, not resisted. He contended that

> it pays to make allies of the forces that, although not morally in our direct line, can accelerate our endeavor. A church planted in a city, a school planted in a thriving center, come more quickly to a large, useful and self-sustaining life than those which try to maintain an existence in rural surroundings. They can command the services of men of enterprise, and who interpret the thought of the hour.[25]

Merrill was sure that "leaders for the next twenty-five years would be found in the cities . . . [and the] best approach to the race is through its leaders. . . . To neglect them is to doom to destruction a race that is preeminently shaped by its leaders."[26] He felt strongly that

the money which [the association] is spending should, so far as possible, represent the opinions of those who give it. It is largely Congregational money. Like very much of this kind of money it is not used to extend Congregationalism. Especially in the work among the Negroes is this true. Just so fast and so far as it is wise, taking into account the interests of the Kingdom of Heaven, to plant Congregational churches, it is done; but, as a matter of fact, we have and shall have to rest content to make as thoroughly Christian as we can those who, as the song has it, are "Baptist and Methodist born, and Baptist and Methodist are to die."

It is casting pearls before swine for our society to do characteristically Congregational church work in the more sparsely settled portions of the South. Not until these regions shall have been enlightened by the bright young men and women who, with a determination wellnigh unmatched, carry thither with much vigor the life of the strong church and school of the centers will such a work as our money represents be possible far from the larger villages, the towns and cities of the South. . . .

The churches of our name have stood for a learned ministry and a thoughtful laity—for an intelligent piety. When we are ready to ignore these distinguishing characteristics of Congregationalism, can we have cheap schools everywhere and a church at every crossroad; but this should not be done until the money for which we are stewards is given by those who have lost their faith in the Congregational Way in matters of education and religion. Until then, it seems to me, the only possible business-like and Christian way is to make strong the centers that we have planted, and from them send forth into all the area that the circumference of these span, the light of an intelligent gospel.[27]

Much enthusiasm was created by Merrill's proposal, and a

great deal of discussion and planning were entered into. To be sure, if the faith of the Puritan ancestors were to remain alive among Blacks in the South, the signs of the changing time must be followed and the cities should become the strategic centers for Congregational missionary endeavors.

After six years of toil, negotiation, and delay, the first child of the city plan was finally given birth. This was the First Congregational Church of Atlanta, Georgia, which emerged from old Storrs School. The First Church of Atlanta was a significant tribute to the denomination. It was believed to be the first "fully equipped" institutional Christian church for Black people in the world. The building was furnished with a gymnasium, model kitchen, sewing room, bathroom, and Sunday school room. It was a handsome, spacious stone structure capable of seating about one thousand people. An ex-mayor of the city of Atlanta, who was present at the dedication of the building in 1908, saluted the church and paid tribute to the congregation and the association for the contribution made to the Black community by both the church and the school. On a visit to the city of Atlanta, the President of the United States, William Howard Taft, was "astonished" when he saw this magnificent edifice for Black people in the heart of the South. And on another occasion President Theodore Roosevelt said of the Atlanta church, "I hail the establishment of a church of this kind, for I feel that you are not only doing the best for the colored people of Atlanta, but also for the people of both races throughout the South."[28]

Indeed, Congregationalists all over the nation and the world were deeply encouraged by the establishment of this church. At the meeting of the National Council in 1910, two years after the dedication of the First Church, the Hon. Thomas C. MacMillan, moderator of the council, brought before the attention of those assembled the fact that

> there are forty cities in the Southern states with twenty thousand or over. In these cities colored brethren are found in numbers. . . . In every one of these cities we should establish and support a church modeled after our splendid First Church in Atlanta, under capable and consecrated leadership.[29]

In 1911, three full years after the completion of the Atlanta structure, no other Black Congregational churches of its kind were built in any other southern city. Many people in the North and the South were concerned about the continued delay. Among these was the Rev. H.H. Proctor of Atlanta, pastor and builder of the first and only answer to the cry for an urban institutional church. With great passion and concern, Proctor wrote that "the time has come for . . . Congregationalists to take a forward step by planting an institutional church for the colored people in the chief cities in the South."[30] He gave four reasons for the urgency of the request and the pressing nature of the need. In the first place, he felt, such churches could socialize the disadvantaged of the Black population and thereby reduce race riots and tension. Second, an "open Congregational Church" could replace the "open saloon," alleviating drunkenness and illegal operations. Further, he was of the opinion that the churches could provide the public facilities that were greatly lacking in all cities throughout the South. Finally, these churches could assist in bridging the gap and in overcoming what he believed to be the operational and organizational deficiencies of the traditional Black church. Proctor urged that such institutional churches be established immediately in Charlotte, North Carolina; Chattanooga and Memphis, Tennessee; Montgomery and Birmingham, Alabama; Little Rock, Arkansas; Dallas, Texas; New Orleans, Louisiana; and Beaufort, South Carolina. He was optimistic and, indeed, faithful enough to believe that $25,000 would be an adequate sum to begin this tremendous but urgent task.

Certainly during this period there were significant developments in the life of the urban Black Congregational churches at Raleigh, Charlotte, Savannah, Louisville, Lexington, Nashville, New Orleans, Memphis, and Birmingham. The impact these churches made fell far short of expectation, however. They were greatly restricted in the "circumference which they spanned."

Chapter 9

"The Marking of Time, a Faint Whimper, and Confused Deliberations"

There were pauses in the process, moments of petrification when the living current was frozen into rigidity. And there was loss of memory; what had gone before was forgotten and men began to move without remembrance of their point of departure or their plan of march.
—H. Richard Niebuhr
The Kingdom of God in America

James M. Gustafson, in his book *Treasure in Earthen Vessels: The Church as a Human Community*, suggests that voluntary missionary societies in America (such as the American Missionary Association) were formed because "the existing structures of denominational life were inadequate" to meet the challenges of the new frontiers.[1] "Voluntary associations outside of the established ecclesiastical patterns were formed, drawing their membership and contributions from various congregations and denominations. For some decades the voluntary missionary association appeared to be an adequate social organization to realize the evangelical task."[2]

Gustafson further points out, however, that "as the mission work became widespread and the complexity of the societies grew . . . a new rational ordering of the political process was necessary." More efficient means for the gathering of contributions and the recruitment of personnel became necessary. Competition among agencies for missionary endeavor for resources in the home churches and for converts on the mission fields is not

87

only keen but a hindering force in the work. This being the case, the relationship of numerous voluntary societies to existing denominational structures had to be set in order. These and other needs fostered patterns of change in the approach of the denominations to missions. Some of the missionary societies became official boards of denominations, while others united to avoid duplication of effort and to achieve a rational division of labor.

> In the course of decades, large "holding companies" came into being, such as the Congregational Board of Home Missions, in which some of the autonomy of the societies is maintained within an efficiently organized general administration. New patterns of political representation developed; rather than hold separate meetings of various societies, the same delegates from churches legislate for all societies.[3]

The American Missionary Association followed very much the same pattern toward bureaucratization that Gustafson outlines. As we indicated in Chapter 3, although the AMA was from its beginning nonsectarian, it was significantly Congregational in its major support, spirit, and orientation. In 1865, when the National Council of Congregational Churches pledged to contribute $250,000 to the budget of the AMA, the slow, "rational ordering of the political process" toward bureaucracy and denominational administrative control was rudimentarily underway.[4]

When the scope of the denomination's home mission work increased, agencies were established to cope with specific areas of concern and need. The functions of the AMA as a society structurally independent of the larger church had always reached into the multifarious phases of the church's mission. It was a composite church building, extension, and evangelical society. It was an agency for emergency relief, reconstruction, and charitable endeavor; a council for social witness and action; and a board of education, both Christian and secular. With the formation of boards and agencies of the denomination which could give expert attention to these multiple needs, practicality led the Congregational churches to take heed of the fact of duplication and to become aware of the possibilities and advantages that bureaucratic specialization availed.[5] This trend marks a significant turning point in the life of the AMA. It was now caught in necessity for the "rational ordering" of denominational structure and would bear the gain or suffer the loss that institutionalism entails.

At the annual meeting of the association, October 22-24, 1912 at Buffalo, New York, two important steps toward institutionalism and denominational coordination were taken.

> First, that the biennial meetings of the Association be held in conjunction with the National Council of Congregational Churches. Second, that, if found expedient, Article Three of the Constitution of the American Missionary Association be amended so as to permit a whole or part of the official delegates to the National Council to become voting members of the Association.[6]

In 1913 the annual meeting of the association was held in conjunction with the National Council at Kansas City, Missouri. At that meeting, "Article Three [was] . . . amended to include as voting members of the Association all the official delegates to the National Council. This amendment virtually placed the Association under the jurisdiction of the National Council, since its official delegates greatly outnumbered the Association's corporate members."[7]

It was in the year 1913, therefore, that the American Missionary Association officially became a part of the increasingly bureaucratic structures of the Congregational churches. In that same year the AMA began to look more critically at its work and to measure the effectiveness of its approach in terms of the standards of the more specialized denominational agencies and boards. In the sixty-seventh annual report of 1913, in an evaluation of its Black church work in the South, the association discovered that

> ordinary Congregational precedents fail in the financial development of their life. Where the National Home Missionary Society probably pays an average of one-third of the support of pastors under its commission the AMA pays two-thirds. The Church Building Society expects to pay not more than one-third of the cost of church buildings in which it assists; this association usually pays two-thirds. In brief, financial proportions have just about to be reversed in our denominational cooperation with these churches.[8]

Perplexed by these statistics, the association pondered the action it should take: "Shall denominational control follow the same proportion [2 to 1 as compared to 1 to 2 for the white churches] or shall the denomination give more money and relatively less control to the Negro churches than to others?"[9]

Increased institutionalism brought the AMA into close proximity with the methods and standards of other denominational agencies to the end that it began to adjust its procedures to the standards, methods, and precedents they set. Despite this fact, however, the association remained partially aware of the unique and pressing problems of its peculiar mission and was fed by the faith, dynamic, and vision of its past. "We believe in the Negro churches as vitally Congregational, and in their development from within. On the other hand, the financial contacts which effect this process include a good many perplexities in which the Association needs sympathy as well as the churches."[10] But, the association warned,

> we cannot escape the profound pedagogic responsibility. Our duty of leadership is just as holy as theirs of self-development. We must stubbornly insist upon vital if not conventional Congregational standards and it is into the reality of freedom, and not its mere semblance, which we are bound to lead this people if we can.[11]

It is somewhat surprising that the annual report of 1913 did not take into account, other than in a "romanticized way," the economic limitations contingent upon the Black populace as a result of practices of discrimination and patterns of segregation in American life. Had this been considered, perhaps there was justification for the reverse ratio between the association's finances and that of the other denominational boards.

Nonetheless, the bureaucratic pressures upon the American Missionary Association made it embarrassingly aware of the "sub-standard" peculiarities of its "appointed task." In this mood it withdrew into the womb of introspection to ponder the requirements placed upon it by the denomination, on the one hand, and the kingdom of God, on the other. The march toward the cities and the cry for leadership that resounded at the beginning of the century were now replaced by the marking of time, a faint whimper, and confused deliberations.

Chapter 10
"Decreasing Demands for Checks from Dad"

When synthesis took the place of dialectic and institutions took the place of movement, the creative time was
past.

—H. Richard Niebuhr
The Kingdom of God in America

Beginning in 1913 and continuing through the present, the
American Missionary Association became a denominational bureau and ceased to be a radical movement within the southern
framework—the framework embracing the new frontier. Nev-
ertheless, there was no doubt in the mind of the AMA that the
demand for its schools was a continuing and urgent necessity.
Although public education for Blacks in the states to the south
had come a long way in the years since the Civil War in both
quantity and quality, it had not kept pace with the sorely pressing
needs of the Deep South in economic, social, and other matters.

In 1918 only 58.1 percent of all the Black children in the South
between the ages of six and fourteen attended schools. This was
by no means a simple matter of lack of ambition or parental
concern. Overcrowded conditions and lack of facilities made it
impossible for them to enroll. The supply was far too inadequate
to meet the demand. The elementary schools in Birmingham,
Alabama could accommodate only 60 percent of the Black children who were of age and had the right to attend.[1] The Atlanta
public schools could provide accommodations for only half the
Black students who waited before their doors. Not even one third
of the Negro children in New Orleans could be cared for in the

schools, and in the rural areas of Alabama, Georgia, and Louisiana the attendance averaged 50 percent, 56 percent, and 30 percent, respectively. Except for a few state agricultural and mechanical colleges and scattered independent institutions, students were dependent on denominational or parochial schools for an approved high school, normal, or college course.

In 1922 Georgia had 1,200,000 Blacks and not one public high school giving fifteen units of credit. The only such Black institution in the entire state was Knox Institute in Athens, Georgia, an AMA school.[2] The state of Alabama had over 1,000,000 Blacks and only four public high schools giving more than twelve units credit. In Alabama the AMA had five such schools, while the state had only four. It was also discovered that more than one half the teachers in and around such metropolitan centers as New Orleans and Memphis were graduates of AMA colleges and normal schools.

The American Missionary Association was able and ready to respond to these educational needs in spite of its place in the new bureaucracy. It had given itself as an agent of a god who specializes, and once again education became the kingdom that it was to establish and control. Appropriations for the association schools greatly increased and greater diligence was rendered in the task. This is not to suggest, however, that more institutions were established or that the field was enlarged. Rather, this is an indication that the schools were coming of age—more adequate and permanent buildings had to be built; faculties enlarged; teachers (who were not now "missionaries") had to be paid in full.[3] The schools, particularly the colleges, continued as flourishing units of the association's witness and work. Indeed, they were as an oasis in the desert of poverty, ignorance, and bigotry in the southern hinterlands.

While enthusiasm for the educational mission increased—or at least held its own—under the disabilities of institutionalism and organizational bureaucracy, the dynamic movement of church establishment greatly waxed and waned. In keeping with the "rational ordering of the political process" trend that commenced in 1913 when the association officially came under denominational control, Black superintendents were appointed to "supervise the field." The first superintendent of southern churches was the Rev. G.W. Moore, who was assisted by "local" or regional superintendents of "field church work."[4] In 1919 the first southern headquarters was established in Atlanta, Georgia, and Alfred K. Lawless was appointed general superintendent of the churches affiliated with the AMA. Henry S. Barnwell, a Talladega College and Seminary graduate, was first assistant to the general superintendent and became superintendent in 1927, after Lawless's death. "Organization," "supervision," "Congregational standards," and "self-support" were the watchwords of those in control.

In 1920, when Fred L. Brownlee became secretary of the AMA, the coordination of its work with that of other denominational boards was almost complete. In reality the churches remained "children" of the association, from whom attention was requested and to whom attention must be paid. Brownlee came to the association at that historic moment when it began to be aware of the apparent failures of its past and to judge itself over against the high standards of the Congregational structures and Way. He was impressed with the problems these struggling churches posed. In what way should he approach his task? Would he be led by the dynamic but frustrating persuasion, power, and direction of the AMA's work in the past, or would he continue the "rational ordering" that bureaucracy precipitates and demands? After careful observation of the churches, Brownlee came to a decision, and his first reactions were these:

> What shall we say about the AMA churches? I have not as yet rallied from the blow of my first impression due to the fact that so few of these churches have come to self-support and self-direction. After 50 years of experience the AMA has brought very few churches to self-support. This is because no association can bring an organization to self-support.
>
> The church that is not fired by the sense of personal responsibility will never become what it should become, be its assistance from the AMA great or small. I do not blame the churches for this failure. So long as a son can write to Dad for a check and Dad is willing to send it, many a son will keep on writing Dad. But the AMA has had its eyes open and it does not mean to sin against the

churches too much longer. Next year is to be a test year. Every church will have set before it a standard that will mark progress toward self-support and larger service; this same standard must also mark a decreasing demand for checks from Dad.[5]

In keeping with this thought and plan of action, four years later, Assistant Superintendent Henry S. Barnwell wrote that "the old thought of looking to a missionary society for leadership and support in those things which a church ought to produce under its own leadership has so weakened the people that they seem incapable of conducting a typical Congregational Church."[6]

In discussing church patterns and institutions that developed after the eighteenth- and nineteenth-century revival movements in America, H. Richard Niebuhr makes an observation that is particularly pertinent to our present discussion of the American Missionary Association. Niebuhr observed that

with the cessation of the [revival] movement and the turn to institutionalism the aggressive societies became denominations, for that peculiar institution, the American denomination, may be described as a missionary order which has turned to the defensive and lost its consciousness of the invisible catholic church. These orders now confused themselves with their cause and began to promote themselves, identifying the kingdom of Christ with the practices and doctrines prevalent in the group. Though the content of the institutionalized faith seemed to be like that of the movement, its spirit was utterly different.[7]

Niebuhr's analysis of the process of institutionalization and "denominationalization" of missionary societies when the movement ceases explains the evolution of the work of the American Missionary Association. It could not, of course, become a separate or new denomination because of its integral and structural relation with the Congregational churches and Way. But with increased bureaucratization or "rational ordering," the dynamic movement ceased. Many new approaches were used in the work. Numerous innovations were made, but none were adequate substitutes for the dynamic and constructive movement that had been the genuine life force of the AMA.

Passion for the work came to a halt. The original impetus or power of the "church-forming revelation" of the association had been depleted or forgotten. The work among the Congregational churches divorced from its original purpose and image separated from the spirit of theocracy, severed from the desire for radical movement and change, and showed itself powerless to summon to new life creative initiative among Blacks in the South. Though the content of the institutionalized faith seemed to be like that of the movement, its spirit was utterly different. With eyes open; with no intention to "sin against the churches"; a test year coming; "standards to be met"; "decreasing" checks from Dad; and ineptitude for "conducting a typical Congregational Church" the spirit of Congregationalism became burdened, anxious, confused. There, on whatever winding path church movements tread, the AMA paused to catch its breath, to be refreshed by the Spirit of God, and to seek the Christian way.

Chapter 11
"The Children Is Crying"

In the year 1864, Jack Blade, an ex-slave of the Seabrook Plantation in South Carolina, addressed a letter to his teacher, the Rev. G.W. Sission of the American Missionary Association. Jack Blade, who had had very little formal education, or "book learning," was a soul of deep vision and longing. In spite of the turmoil of his time and in spite of his memory of a bitter past as a slave, he could nonetheless believe in the confusing signs and portents of his present and hope in a full but uncertain future. Blade's letter to his teacher speaks for itself and is worthy of our recording here:

August 1, 1864

My dear Brother Sission:

I now sit down with greate pleasure to inform you these few lines, hoping this letter may find you again, in the state of good health; so when you go home, you may make up your mind and come again in the winter when it is cold. We all are very sorry that your health prove so badly, so that you was obliged to go; but we all are in good hope that as soon as the winter come again, and the wether is cold, we all will like very much to have you come back.

I hope you may remember our little pray meeting, which we have held together in the name of the Lord, and if things be so that you cannot come back, I hope we may remember one another in the name of the Lord; so that if we never meet again in this life; I hope we may meet again in heaven.

But no doubt perhaps, when you look and see this one of you poore scholars handwriting, perhaps you may say one of these days, I think I will make up my mind and go back no more.

I go to say something to Miss Ann [the wife of Rev. Sission], I want to tell her the little children is crying everyday, asking me, "Father, where is Miss Ann? I want my lesson." So I tell them to cry on and perhaps it may go North, and one of these nights, Miss Ann may dream a dream, and when she see that, she come back again. . . . I am very sorry that my writing is so bad, but I have no light to see by and it is night. No more to say at this present time.

Mr. Jack Blade

A century and a decade have passed since Jack Blade penned this letter. Yet, his plea, which is the current longing of many a human heart, remains the essential challenge to the church, the company of God.

In earlier chapters we have sought to locate the moments, the situation, or (as H. Richard Niebuhr describes them) the "church-forming, community-building revelations" in the history of Congregationalism in America that determined the nature of its response to the Black South just before, during, and after the Civil War. We have also attempted to show how the success and failure of this denomination on the new frontier of the Freedmen was directly related to the institutional image and the historic idea of the spirit of Congregationalism that it continued to exemplify.

In the mid-1920s, however, when Congregationalism sought to establish itself as a bureaucratized religion of the cultured and the sophisticated, it lost its spontaneity. It lost the vitality that caused it to dare and abandoned its previous sense of mission as irrelevant to the well-being of a successful church. Although many Black Congregational churches in the South survived this abandonment of the denomination's original sense of mission on the Black frontier, Congregationalism as a dynamic movement ceased because the weaknesses of its image and vital form, the weaknesses of its Pilgrim and Puritan heritage, exceeded its strengths. The aggressiveness in mission that issues from the dialectic created by the tension of what is and what ought to be could no longer be sustained. Congregationalism as a vital movement in southern Negro life ceased when the denomination could no longer envision the Black South as a new, challenging frontier, when the frontier dimension of its task was no longer regarded as urgent. Congregationalism as a vital movement in the Black South came to a halt when the active channels through which this church could listen and respond to the "children's cry" were tightly closed by bureaucratic establishment, by demands for success as conceived by distorted images of what the church should be, and by racial and cultural prejudices thinly disguised as the Congregational theocratic ideal.

Church history can be written and read from two different but proper perspectives. One is to re-create and restore as objectively as possible all the data relevant to the history of a particular church or to a special aspect of it. This involves research and interpretation, relating sets of data to each other in the sequence of events narrated. Reading church history in this manner brings a store of information about the past life of the Christian community. Events can be placed in proper chronological order and can be seen in relation to corresponding events in general history.

On the other hand, church history can be written to re-create the story of the life and thought of the community in such a way as to foster an understanding of the community's inner dynamic. The readers can understand what the events meant to the actors and what are the meaningful implications of these events for later development. Thus the history of the church becomes not only an external collection of data but also an inner understanding of the meaning of events that have shaped the community. Not only can readers of that history develop a factual ordering of data, but they can also project themselves into the history. They are able to see its significance not only for the church in a particular time and place but for the present as well. In this way, the identification with the past, through its moments of great consequence for the church, becomes inner and subjective in character. In effect, the history is inwardly appropriated.

It is largely in keeping with this latter intention of writing church history that this book has been written. It has been our particular concern that the readers of this critical rehearsal of the history of Congregationalism among Black people in the South should project themselves into this history in such a way that they gather an active understanding of its inner dynamic, inwardly appropriate it, and respond to this history in terms of its significance for discovering the present challenges that summon both the church and themselves.

As we view the history of Congregationalism among Blacks in the South from this inner perspective, there is much about which we can speak in praise. It is indeed possible for one to salute Congregationalism in a very special way for having seen from the outset that the roots of the so-called "Black problem" in America did not lie in innate characteristics or in genetic deficiencies of Black people. The earliest missionaries of the American Missionary Association operated on the assumption that the Freedmen's problems were generated by their acquired attitudes and the lifestyle imposed upon them by the dehumanizing circumstances of slavery. For the early Congregational missionaries, what they presumed to be the Black people's problem was to be found not in the Black's natural intellectual and physical endowment but in the Black's culture and history. Documents at our disposal never once indicate that agents acting on behalf of the American Missionary Association advocated the intellectual or biological inferiority of Blacks.

Certainly, in regard to this position these Congregationalists were far ahead of their time, for this approach to the race problem (pointing to history rather than biology as the source of the "Black problem") did not become the approach of American politics and higher education until well into the twentieth century. In spite of this, it must be noted that the Congregational view of the history of the problem of the American Negro was dreadfully limited. The Congregational view of the Black problem was limited for it asserted that the roots of this American dilemma were to be found solely in the history of slavery and segregation. What the representatives of Congregationalism deleted from their view was the fact that Congregationalism and Congregationalists were in a real sense collaborators in a culturally conditioned social and historic perspective, however innocently entertained, that contributed no little amount to the forging of the Negro problem. White Americans particularly, and Europeans generally, have been reluctant to admit that cultural supremacy is the underside of white supremacy. This has been especially true when cultural supremacy could be obscured in some ideological framework which gave it sanction that made this framework appear to be absolute and divine.

What was particularly true for Americans and generally true for Europeans was also true for these Congregationalists. Early Congregationalists working among Blacks in the South had little regard for African history and culture. Also, they were not always able to distinguish between those negative aspects of the Black character that were shaped by the indignities of slavery, on the one hand, and those positive aspects that were blended out of the rich African past and the more wholesome aspects of the American experience, on the other. The product the early Congregationalist sought to achieve with the rigorously humane approach to the education of the Freedman was, in fact, modeled upon the New England gentleman. The slightest residue in this process of the Freedman's African past was not given favorable recognition by the Congregational school and church. The Congregational theocratic ideal became "cultural arrogance" when it lost touch with that inner corrective which is sustained only when people remain aware that human effort predicated upon premises that are themselves limited or partisanly conditioned in any degree can often create the very problems it purports to solve.

In this sense, then, the attempt of Congregationalists to educate the Negroes often led to their miseducation. In this sense, the effort of Congregationalists to "Christianize" the Negroes, whenever successful, frequently made for their despiritualization. The "cultural arrogance" of the Congregational missionaries combined with their deep dedication and missionary zeal to produce educators who were not generally aware of their own need to be educated in the rich tradition and culture of Afro-America, a tradition that justifiably sought inclusion in any religious or cultural synthesis. It is thus something of a paradox how this "cultural arrogance" employed as vehicle the missionaries' own deep devotion to solve the problems of the Black frontier, producing evangelists who were not aware that the Spirit comes upon diverse people in many cultural forms.

As we study the failure of Congregationalism to establish itself as a church in the Black South, it is interesting to note that whenever Congregationalism focused attention on the failure of the Black churches it almost always sought to locate this failure in the cultural and religious deficiencies inherent in the Black experience and in the Black leadership of these churches. Emissaries of the New England Congregational church took little account of and often had little appreciation for the success of the independent Black churches and their leaders, whose impact upon the Black community, whose ability to appeal to the Black masses, and whose ability to concretize and dignify the Black religious experience have in so many instances been substantial and sincere. The Black churches of Congregationalism were what they were because Congregationalists were who they were. The weaknesses of these churches were due as much to the problems and pressures of white culture as to the problems and pressures of Black culture. The failure of these churches can surely be attributed to the lack of responsible Black leadership. But the church does not profit from its own history unless it also concedes that the failure of these churches was due also to the lack of responsible white leadership—a leadership capable of recognizing the relativities of its own culture and the limitations of its own experience in the faith.

Despite the ultimately heroic enterprise of education of Freedmen by self-giving New England whites, history was later to disclose that one of the major causes for the failure of Congregationalism among Blacks in the South could be that the liberalism and openness of the spirit of Congregationalism was not really liberal and open enough in the context of the twentieth century. This spirit, when uprooted from the soil of New England culture and transplanted in the Black South, became grounded in the inequities and paternalism that emerge when any group attempts to control another people's destiny and corporate life. It was this very perversion that found nourishment in a cultural arrogance misconceived as a theocratic ideal.

It would be tempting and perhaps popular to conclude that in the final analysis the powers that be in Congregationalism abandoned its church-forming efforts among Blacks not because they were poor, uneducated, and emotional but simply because they were Black. But to yield to this temptation would be to condemn too easily what must have been very complex motivations and to judge too harshly the many moments, places, and persons in which these motivations were sincere, earnest, pure.

Yet, it must be said that at a time in which it is fashionable to regard racism as an impersonal system, the history of Congregationalism among Blacks in the South must indeed remind us that prejudice against other human beings, however benignly or innocently expressed, spawns inevitable consequences that belie the fact of genuinely creative interchange between persons.

Perhaps the deep-going insecurity of white Americans in their relation to nonwhite aspirations has been clearly exposed once and for all when during the 1960s Blacks exposed America's hypocrisy and cultural arrogance and petitioned whites for an equal place in the sun. In an organized, independent, aggressive assertion of strength, Blacks determined to push beyond the limits of what the white brokers of culture, religion, and power could produce for them and to set out on their own, not merely to survive but to be fully human, to be fully free. The Black community in America today is undergoing one of the most strange metamorphoses in the history of humankind. It is experiencing an epoch of change, turbulence, disquietude, unrest, and the familiar pain that inevitably accompany revolution and growth.

Lerone Bennett has suggested that the real problem in race relations in America is not the so-called Black problem but the "white problem." Only when white America is able to face its own insecurities, its own personal and social anxieties, and its own frustrations and self-hatred can we begin the long, hard tasks of a new reconstruction in American race relations. In this context, then, liberation is indeed the task of the American churches —liberation both of Blacks and of whites. The realities of twentieth-century American life give evidence of the enslavement of both races. Blacks and whites are oppressed. Both long to be free.

At a time such as this, when Black change seems so radical, signs must not be lacking, then, of white change and white growth too. For anything that hides white America from the need for confrontation with itself and from the fact that white America must change before it can effectively deal with Black change hides the harsh realities and responsibilities of the most serious and pressing dimensions of the American churches' new frontier in race relations.

Indeed, at such a time as this, when the Congregational spirit, as this has been historically disclosed at its finest, is so painfully absent in the motivation and design of contemporary ecclesiastical outreach, we must make haste to reinstate with all deliberate speed those proven dynamics of the Puritan ancestors, moving in whatever new ways the needs of this strange time and the needs of this strange new racial frontier demand.

The Congregational churches were among the first to come to the aid of the emancipated Negro, bringing with them the gifts of education and the redeeming word of the gospel of Jesus Christ. Although the United Church of Christ (of which union the Congregational churches are a part) may not prove to be the ultimate instrument through which the Congregational spirit shall take on new life and move toward the emancipation and liberation of all Americans, Black and white, those persons who are the true heirs of the Congregational legacy stand in a unique position to face the challenge of the new racial frontier of white and Black liberation which has presently emerged and which summons the American church to act and to be. As H. Richard Niebuhr has indicated, "the same institutionalism which represents the death of an old movement can, as history amply illustrates, become the pregnant source of a new aggression. It cannot be otherwise with a church which conserves in some form the Gospel of the Kingdom of God."[1] Indeed, the "children," Black and white, are crying every day. The real heirs of the Congregational Way fail if with diligence they do not respond to every person's need to be liberated, set free.

The Rev. Joseph Edwin Roy
(1827–1908)

The Rev. Joseph Edwin Roy (1827–1908) became Field Secretary for the AMA in 1878. This Field Office was in Atlanta. While in this position, Roy led in the organization of fifty Congregational churches for Blacks in the South. In 1885 the association appointed him District Secretary, with offices in Chicago.

The Rev. Samuel Coles

The Rev. Samuel Coles, a graduate of Talladega College, served as a missionary in Angola, West Africa. In addition to being an able preacher and pastor, Coles was an expert in agriculture and in ironworks. Because he taught the African people served by the Angola Mission to make farm tools from native deposits of iron ore, he became known on the mission field as "The Preacher with a Plough." Coles was supported by the diligence of his wife, Bertha, also a graduate of Talladega College.

The Rev. and Mrs. Henry C. McDowell and son Curtis

Dr. and Mrs. McDowell were among the first missionaries sent to the denomination's mission in Angola, West Africa. A part of the AMA's initial intention was to "evangelize the Colored Race in America for the Christianization of Africa." Few American Blacks went as missionaries to Africa, choosing, rather, to remain in America and to serve the needs of their people who were closer at hand. Dr. McDowell also distinguished himself as pastor of Dixwell Congregational church in New Haven, Connecticut (the oldest Black Congregational Church in America, established in 1820); as principal of Lincoln Academy, an AMA school at Kings Mountain, North Carolina; and as founding pastor of the Open Door Congregational Church in Miami, Florida. Dr. McDowell is a graduate of Talladega College.

The Rev. Orishatukeh Faduma
(1907)
The Rev. Orishatukeh Faduma
(1907), a native of Sierra Leone,
pastored churches in North Carolina.

The Rev. J.M. Robinson
The Rev. and Mrs. J.M. Robinson
served for eighteen years (1892–
1910) as principal and teacher respectively at the Brewer Normal
School in Greenwood, South Carolina.

Mrs. J.M. Robinson

Harriet I. Miller
From her home in Wisconsin, Harriet I. Miller went to Atlanta in 1885, where she became principal of the AMA's prestigious Storrs School. In 1888 she went to Meridian, Mississippi, and became the founding principal of the Lincoln School.

Gregory Congregational Church, Wilmington, North Carolina (1901). The Gregory School was part of the Wilmington Mission.

The Old Mid-Way Church, Liberty County, Georgia. In this building, prior to the Civil War, Blacks worshiped in the balcony. This building still stands and has been designated as a Historical Landmark by the National Park Services of the U.S. Department of the Interior.

Second Congregational Church, Memphis, Tennessee (1892).

Midway Congregational Church, Liberty County, Georgia (1910). The establishment of this church took a different form from that of most southern Congregational churches for Blacks. It emerged from the old Mid-Way Congregational Church in Liberty County, Georgia. Before the Civil War, Blacks worshiped in the gallery of the white congregation. After the war, Blacks established their own church, generously assisted by whites of the old Mid-Way Church and of Liberty County. The Black church was related to the Dorchester Academy and shared a campus with it. The church shown here has been replaced by a more modern structure.

Fisk Memorial Chapel, Fisk University (1900), home of the famous Fisk University Jubilee Singers. The chorus took the folk melodies of the Black South to northern United States and Europe.

First Congregational Church, Atlanta, Georgia (1909). The visit of President William Howard Taft, Atlanta, Georgia (1909). First Congregational Church in Atlanta was the first Black church in America to build an institutional church structure. Its membership included some of the wealthiest, most prestigious Blacks of Atlanta; many of them were free persons before the Civil War. The Rev. Henry Hugh Proctor, then pastor of First Church, is shown standing to the left of President-elect Taft. The banner reads:

MR. TAFT:

THE FIRST INSTITUTIONAL CHURCH IN THE HEART OF THE SOUTH FOR THE COLORED RACE GREETS YOU AND WISHES YOU GODSPEED.

This building still stands in downtown Atlanta.

Graduates of the Talladega College Seminary (ca. 1909). Students at American Missionary Association College seminars served as pastors of nearby Congregational churches.

A mission Sunday school (ca. 1909) of the Shelby, Alabama Congregational Church. The Rev. O.W. Hawkins, pastor of the Shelby Church, is on the right.

The Christian Endeavor Orchestra of Central Congregational Church of New Orleans (1905) is indicative of the cultural aspirations and achievements of those who came under the influence of the association.

Ballard Normal School and First Congregational Church in Macon, Georgia (1890). The Ballard School was one of many AMA schools and properties eventually given to states, counties, or cities as an incentive for them to provide public education for Blacks.

The parsonage of the Congregational Church, Augusta, Georgia (1921). AMA teachers and ministers taught their students and congregations the value of property ownership. Often the parsonages and teachers' homes were used as models for Black aspirations.

The Talladega College Choir entering DeForest Chapel (1920). The cultural, moral, and spiritual development of students was the primary task of the AMA church and school.

Appendix A: Tables

Table I
**Ten Most-productive Missionary Societies in
America, 1869**

American Board of Foreign Missions	$535,838
American Missionary Association*	300,508
American Bible Society	248,160
American Home Missionary Society	217,577
American Tract Society	118,773
American Sunday School Union	98,505
American Female Guardian Society	65,540
American Congregational Union	59,848
American Seaman's Friend Society	55,382
American Colonization Society	53,190

*AMA sum does not include $50,000 in clothing and supplies.

Table II
**Negro Population and Percentage of Total
Population in the United States—1790-1940**

Year	Population	Percentage
1790	757,000	19.3
1840	2,874,000	16.8
1860	4,442,000	14.1
1890	7,489,000	11.9
1920	10,463,000	9.9
1940	12,800,000	9.7

Table III
Carey's Estimates of the Number of Slaves
Imported into the United States at Various
Time Periods*

Time Period	No. Slaves Imported	Average Import Per Year
Prior to 1715	30,000	—
1715-50	90,000	2,500
1751-60	35,000	3,000
1761-70	74,500	7,400
1771-90	34,000	1,700
1791-1888	70,000	3,900
Total	333,500	

*See Henry C. Carey, *The Slave Trade* (Philadelphia, 1853), p. 18.

Table IV
Location and Number of AMA Schools by
July 1871*

Location	Number	Location	Number
District of Columbia	2	Tennessee	16
Maryland	4	Kentucky	62
Delaware	2	Iowa	2
Virginia	51	Illinois	14
North Carolina	17	Missouri	13
South Carolina	12	Kansas	3
Georgia	41	Arkansas	17
Florida	7	Louisiana	21
Alabama	16	Texas	15
Mississippi	28		
		Total	343

*These were originally temporary schools; many had already been discontinued by 1871.

Table V
Summary Statistics of AMA Work Among
Freedmen—First Decade, 1861-71

Expenditure: Clothing and Supplies—estimated cash
value for 7 years (no account kept
for first 3 years) $381,173.87

Expenditure: Missionaries', superintendents', and
teachers' salaries and traveling expenses; land, schools, buildings,
furniture, books, and church buildings 1,841,324.96

    Total expenditure for 10-year period $2,222,498.83

Missionaries and Teachers: Total number commissioned in
10-year period   3,470

Students: In day schools   164,723
           In night schools   156,376
                               Total   324,569

Table VI
Summary Statistics of AMA Educational
Activities, Summit Year, 1871

Schools
Chartered Institutions of Learning   7
Graded and Normal Schools   16
Common Schools   147
    Total   170

Value of School Property $555,500

Students
Day Schools   19,500
Night Schools   2,348
Sabbath Schools   16,254
    Total   38,102

Table VII
Black Congregationalism, 1882-91*

	'82	'83	'84	'85	'86	'87	'88	'89	'90	'91
Missionaries	91	100	104	119	127	103	102	113	107	128
Teachers	213	—	319	250	238	246	266	260	340	373
Churches	83	89	95	112	124	127	131	136	128	138
Membership	5,641	5,974	6,420	6,881	7,571	7,896	9,055	8,438	8,416	8,258
Schools	57	62	65	56	53	54	58	60	80	80
Pupils	9,608	9,640	9,758	8,823	8,753	8,616	9,896	10,094	13,395	13,845
Theological Students	72	70	73	96	118	78	87	82	83	73
Scholars: Church and Mission Sunday Schools	7,835	9,406	13,150	10,569	13,149	15,109	17,023	14,735	17,032	15,931

*Based on the annual reports of the American Missionary Association.

Table VIII
Black and Mulatto Population, 1850-1910*

Census Year	Negro Population Total	Black	Mulatto	Percent of Total Black	Mulatto
1910	9,827,763	7,777,077	2,050,686	79.1	20.9
1890	7,470,040	6,337,980	1,132,060	84.8	15.2
1870	4,880,009	4,295,960	584,049	88.0	12.0
1860	4,441,830	3,853,467	588,363	86.8	13.2
1850	3,638,810	3,233,059	405,751	88.8	11.2

*Monroe N. Work, *Negro Year Book*—1921-22 (Tuskegee Institute, Ala., 1922), p. 379.

Table IX
Negro College Graduates*

Decade	Number of Negro College Graduates
1820-1829	3
1830-1839	Unknown
1840-1849	7
1850-1859	12
1860-1869	44
1870-1879	313
1880-1889	738
1890-1899	1,126
1900-1909	1,613

Ibid., p. 243.

Table X
Number of Negroes in Each Main Class of
Occupation*

Occupation	1910	1900	Increase Number	Percent
Agricultural Pursuits	2,893,674	2,143,176	750,498	35
Professional Service	69,929	41,324	28,605	47
Domestic and Personal Service	1,324,160	1,099,715	224,445	17
Trade & Transportation	425,043	209,154	215,889	103
Mfg. & Mechanical Pursuits	704,174	275,149	429,025	156

*Ibid., p. 313.

	1866	1926	Gain
onomic Progress			
mes Owned	12,000	700,000	688,000
ms Owned	20,000	1,100,000	1,080,000
inesses Conducted	2,100	70,000	67,900
alth Accumulated	$20,000,000	$2,000,000,000	$1,980,000,000
icational Progress			
cent Literate	10	90	80
leges and Normal Schools	15	500	485
dents in Public Schools	100,000	2,150,000	2,050,000
chers in All Schools	600	48,000	47,400
perty for Higher Ed.	$60,000	$40,000,000	$39,940,000
ual Expenditures for			
ducation	$700,000	$37,000,000	$36,300,000
sed by Negroes	$80,000	$3,000,000	$2,920,000
gious Progress			
nber of Churches	700	47,000	46,3000
nbers	600,000	5,000,000	4,400,000
day Schools	1,000	46,000	45,000
day School Pupils	50,000	3,000,000	2,950,000
ue Church Property	$1,500,000	$100,000,000	$98,500,000

., 1925-26.

Table XII
Number and Percent of Negroes
in the South Living in Urban
and Rural Communities, 1890-1910*

| Year | Number | | Percent | | Increase | Decrease |
	Urban	Rural	Urban	Rural	in Urban	in Rural
1890	1,033,235	5,727,342	15.3	84.7		
1900	1,364,796	6,558,173	17.2	82.8	1.9	1.9
1910	1,854,455	6,894,972	21.2	78.8	4.0	4.0

*Ibid., *1915-16*, p. 350.

Table XIII
Percent Increase of Negroes in the
South in Rural and Urban Communities,
1890-1910*

	Urban	Rural
Increase 1890-1900	32.0	14.5
Increase 1900-1910	35.8	5.1

*Ibid., p. 351.

mber and Percent of Negroes in the United
tes Living in Urban and Rural
mmunities*

ar	Number		Percent		Increase in Urban Population	Decrease in Rural Population
	Urban	Rural	Urban	Rural		
0	1,481,142	6,007,534	19.4	80.6		
0	2,005,972	6,828,022	22.7	77.3	2.8 (1890-1900)	2.8 (1890-1900)
0	2,689,229	7,138,534	27.4	72.6	4.7 (1900-1910)	4.7 (1900-1910)

d.

Table XV
Percent Increase of Negroes in the United
States in Urban and Rural Communities,
1890-1910*

	Urban	Rural
Increase 1890-1900	35.4	13.6
Increase 1900-1910	34.0	4.5

*Ibid.

Table XVI
Annual Expenditures for Public Schools by States, 1914*

	Total Expenditures		Percent Expenditures		Percent of Total Population		Average Expenditure per Child of School Age	
	Whites	Negroes	Whites	Negroes	Whites	Negroes	Whites	Negroes
Alabama	$3,396,639	$491,954	87	13	57.5	42.5	8.50	1.49
Arkansas	3,377,549	460,000	88	12	71.8	28.1	7.89	2.62
Florida	2,029,899	297,495	87	13	58.9	41.0	14.75	3.10
Georgia	4,467,185	627,245	88	12	54.9	45.1	9.18	1.42
Kentucky	5,597,199	553,569	91	9	88.6	11.4	8.63	6.45
Louisiana	5,051,345	351,801	93	7	56.8	43.1	16.60	1.59
Mississippi	2,236,571	569,990	80	20	43.7	56.2	8.20	1.53
North Carolina	3,450,375	627,744	85	15	68.0	31.6	6.69	2.50
South Carolina	2,247,981	361,785	86	14	44.8	55.2	9.65	1.09
Tennessee	4,887,029	670,000	88	12	78.3	21.7	8.32	3.94
Texas	11,656,305	1,897,537	86	14	82.2	17.7	10.89	7.50
Virginia	4,350,623	727,419	86	14	67.4	32.6	10.92	3.43

*Ibid., 1914-15.

le XVII
nber of Negro Schools, Teachers, and
dents in Denominational Institutions,
4-15*

rd	Number of Schools	Number of Teachers	Number of Students
erican Baptist	24	408	7,351
gregational	65	587	12,097
scopal	8	131	1,958
sbyterian, U.S.A.	136	444	16,427
ted Presbyterian	17	139	4,261
ciples	6	33	507
thodist Episcopal	22	479	6,588

ed on reports in the *American Missionary.*

Table XVIII
Annual Expenditures, etc., for Negro Education by Certain Religious Boards, 1917-18*

Boards	Current Expenses	Buildings	Permanent Funds for Negro Education	Value of School Plants	Contributed by Patrons Exclusive of Expenditures for Board
American Baptist Home Mission Society	$198,451	$150,000	$388,377	$2,500,000	$20,000
AMA	303,595		2,063,397	1,744,820	
American Church Institute for Negroes (Episcopal)	102,233		116,524	1,023,000	22,213
Board of Missions for Freedmen					

Christ (Disciples)	35,000			276,000	
Board of Education for Negroes of Methodist Episcopal Church	118,159			354,725	
Board of Colored Missions (Evangelical Lutheran Synodical Conference of North America)	45,000	5,000	6,500	90,000	4,000

*Ibid.

Table XIX
Expenditures of AMA Increase*

	1917	1921
Southern	$299,395	$553,651
Indian	31,426	43,710
Oriental	18,633	31,243
Puerto Rico	17,602	33,998
Mountain Work	39,562	43,907

American Missionary, vol. 76 (December 1922), p. 464.

Table XX
Development of AMA During 75 Years of Its History*

Year	Total Income
1846-7	$11,328.27
1856-7	41,190.97
1866-7	334,452.59
1876-7	306,099.95
1886-7	426,589.02
1896-7	401,871.08
1906-7	555,281.91
1916-17	660,222.88
1920-21	947,798.99

(Income of each tenth year; these sums include endowments.)
American Missionary, vol. 76 (November 1921), p. 334.

Appendix B: State Associations and Conferences Whose Resolutions to Support AMA in 1864 Were Included in *American Missionary* Article, Volume 8, August 1864

*1. General Association of Massachusetts meeting in Springfield
 2. The Rhode Island Congregational Conference
 3. The New London (Connecticut) Association of Congregational Ministers
 4. The Litchfield (Connecticut) Association
 5. The Tolland (Connecticut) Association
 6. Windham (Connecticut) Association
 7. Brookfield (Massachusetts) Conference
 8. New Orleans Ministerial Association (Interdenominational)

Sample Resolutions:
A. Rhode Island Congregational Conference:
    Whereas, the American Missionary Association is devoting itself largely to the instruction and evangelization of the Freedmen of the South.

    Resolved, that the Rhode Island Congregational Conference cordially commends the association to the churches as our agent, under Providence, for the prosecution of this work.

B. New Orleans Ministerial Association:
    In the May session, 1864, of the New Orleans Ministerial Association, composed of ministers of several denominations, the following resolution was unanimously adopted:

    Resolved, that we heartily welcome the delegates of the American Missionary Association to this department as co-

---

*1-7 Congregational.

119

laborers in the cause of religion and take occasion to approve the endeavor it is making in behalf of the education of the Race whose cause it has so faithfully pled in the past, and to whom it would now present the priceless boon of social and religious elevation.

Appendix C: Central Congregational Church, New Orleans—Accounts from the *American Missionary*, 1872-1918

Central Congregational Church, New Orleans*

(Reverend S.S. Ashley furnishes us with the subjoined reliable and encouraging account of the recently organized church which worships in the substantial brick edifice lately purchased by the colored people of New Orleans, aided by a loan from the AMA.)

The St. James Church (Methodist Church) disappears henceforth from the roll. In its place stands the "CENTRAL CONGREGATIONAL CHURCH," of good material, well organized, with a large congregation and a flourishing Sabbath school. Reverend Dr. C.H. Thompson will be pastor. The indications are that this church will soon be a power for Christ in this city, both as to order and piety. Needy immortal souls throng through the vicinity of its place of worship.

This enterprise at Liberty street is greatly attracting the attention of the Christian public of this city and is regarded as a pattern. Ministers from other churches come to see how things are done; singers come from the choirs of other churches to hear and see for themselves how Congregational singing is managed; the superintendents and teachers of other Sabbath schools come to its Sabbath school to be enlightened as to Sabbath school methods. From this Church we hope that soon Christian men and women will go out to labor with and strengthen the smaller churches of this city.

---

*Vol. 16 (August 1872), p. 182.

Central Church, Reverend C.H. Thompson, D.D., Pastor,* occupies in the City a pleasant, commodious, and centrally located house of worship, purchased under the auspices of the American Missionary Association.

The Church was organized in May, 1872, and is really a reconstruction of the St. James Congregational Church [St. James was the largest Negro Methodist Church in the City of New Orleans in 1962]. The St. James Church heretofore reported as under the pastoral care of Reverend J.A. Norager, now disappears from our rolls.

Ten members have been added since its [Central's] organization; the present number of members is 45. The increase might have been larger but caution has been exercised as to the qualification of candidates. Purity and consistency of life as the Gospel enjoins, have been required as conditions of its membership.

The Sabbath school numbers 100 and is under the superintendence of Professor J.A. Marthing of Straight University. The Sabbath-night congregation averages about 350 and is increasing. One case of conversion is that of a young man who was reared a Roman Catholic. He was brought to a knowledge of the truth by attending the services of this Church. Many of the Congregation are Roman Catholics, or occasional attendants at Romanish worship; such seem to be interested bearers of the Word.

This church is evidently accomplishing a work among the Romanists of the city that is not effected by other Protestant churches—thus meeting the pressing religious necessity of this community.

It is the opinion of Dr. Thompson that the influence and power of Romanism over the colored people of New Orleans is not increasing and that papal proselyting does not meet with encouraging success.

Dr. Thompson, in addition to pastoral duty, conducts the exercises of the theological class in [Straight] University.

---

*Vol. 17 (May 1873), p. 105.

A Precious Ingathering—The Revival Continued*

—From Reverend W.S. Alexander, New Orleans—

(The Central Church in New Orleans had been for some time without a pastor, but last autumn, Reverend Mr. Alexander assumed pastoral charge, and at once a new interest was awakened, which soon deepened into a blessed revival . . . [Ed. Note].)

The revival in Central Church, of which I wrote you in March, has been in uninterrupted progress since and the interest is still very deep and tender, with a larger number of inquirers than any previous intervals with a large attendance, and all under the power of the Holy Spirit. These meetings have been marked, on the part of Christians, by an earnest desire for a higher, holier consecration, and by great willingness and eagerness to do everything in their power to aid in the Lord's work; and on the part of the unconverted by the clearest conviction of sin, which gave them no rest till they were led intelligently and believingly to Christ.

The decided evidences of God's convicting and converting grace for which I have always longed in my ministry, in precious seasons like this, have here been given, with hardly an exceptional case.

There has been no instance of professed conversion marked by mere emotion and sympathy which would create a suspicion of its genuineness, but under God's guiding hand all have been led step by step into the Kingdom.

As an illustration of this fact, I may mention the experience of a bright intelligent girl of seventeen, who thought that she had fully consecrated herself to the redeemer, and was examined and approved as a candidate for church membership. On the Sabbath morning when the others came forward, she said she "was not worthy," and her admission was delayed. She is now an earnest inquirer, taking the inquirer's seat (the "anxious" bench) at ev-

---

*Vol. 20 (June 1876), pp. 129-30.

ery meeting, and at our Thursday night service she said to me with a flood of tears, "I will come to no more meetings, but stay in my room until I have found peace in my Saviour."

Another, a member of the Board of Trustees, was under the deepest conviction for many days. I thought I had seen strong men weep, but really I never did until I saw this noble man. Tear drops like the summer rain fell from his eyes to the floor, night after night. His eyes were constantly swollen with weeping. But at last, light broke in upon his burdened soul, and from that hour his peace has been like the peace of the river, so deep and full, "the peace of God which passeth all understanding."

Sunday, March 26th was the Day of Our Precious Ingathering

On the Thursday night preceding our preparatory service, the candidates presented themselves for examination. It was an open examination in the presence of the Church and Congregation. Each one, from the dear boy of twelve to the man and woman of forty, stood up, as their names were called, and told "what the Lord had done for their souls." God made all of our hearts tender, and tears of gratitude and joy were mingled with the tears of these converts, "newly born" into the Redeemer's Kingdom.

The morning of the Sabbath was peaceful and beautiful. The congregation which gathered was large, and deeply impressed with the occasion. After two beautiful children had been consecrated to God in baptism, twenty-three adults came forward to take the vows of God upon them. Six were received by letter; and seventeen on profession of their faith in the Redeemer, nine of whom received baptism. Eight were members of Straight University. After they had given their assent to a "creed" and the "covenant," the Right Hand of Fellowship was given, and we sat down together at the table of our Lord. This precious Sabbath has passed into our memories as one of the brightest and best of our lives.

And the good work goes on. Since Communion day, March 26, seventeen decided cases of conversion have occurred, and the number of inquirers, all earnest, and some I believe, very near the light, already reaches thirty. Many are students of the University, where they have daily prayer meetings, and where the teachers are untiring in their devotion and faithfulness.

I have many things in my heart, I would like to say, but hope that what I have said will awaken an earnest spirit of prayer among all the friends of this Southern work, that the revival may not cease till the Church can rejoice over a "mighty ingathering of souls."

God only knows how urgently the whole Southland needs a spiritual baptism. Let us pray for it and work for it!

Revival News—"Pray for My Child"—Older Converts—Romanists Reached*
—Mrs. T.N. Chase, New Orleans Central Church—

You will rejoice to hear of the good work in the Central Congregational Church in New Orleans. The interest has been sufficient to bring an unusual number every night for four weeks to our prayer meeting. One evening, after the pastor had taken nearly the usual time, he called for brief testimony from Christians. Fifty-three responded in the limited half hour.

The fruit to be gathered in was from among the older students of the school, who were not already professing Christians. This was what would be expected by those who were their faithful, Christian teachers. All teachers know the thrilling interest that centers around the conversion of young persons around their tuition (meaning school). So, as I have heard our teachers talk of this scholarly young man, and that promising young woman, coming over to the Lord's side, I know very well what a burden of prayer and effort was lifted from their hearts and hands.

The 3rd week of our meetings a younger class seemed interested. One evening a widow begged us to pray for her daughter in tones that would have melted the heart of a stone. As she passed out of the door at the close of the meeting, I overheard her saying to one and another, "Pray for my child! Pray for my child!" An earnest mother, I thought, who can doubt the reality of her religion? On my way home I learned that her husband had been a devoted member of our church, and a wealthy, intelligent colored citizen. I am happy to find such men are not rare in New Orleans. The next evening the mother, with the same pleading earnestness, begged us to pray for her child. The grandmother was present, too, and gave us a soul stirring testimony of her long pilgrimage. When those who wished our prayers were requested to come

---

*Vol. 32 (April 1878), pp. 113–14.

forward, several responded. All were strangers to me; but when a certain little girl went forward behind the others, and I, for a moment, wondered at my tears. Then it flashed upon me that she must be the widow's child, and my emotion was caused by the flood of sympathy that was involuntarily surging from heart to heart from that praying mother. On inquiry, I found I was not mistaken. You can imagine, better than I can describe, the scene, when mother and grandmother gathered about the child, pleading with her to yield to Jesus, as we all knelt to commend the last lambs to a loving shepherd.

Now, the older people are being reached. Friday night a man came in late to escort his wife home. Saturday he came early, and at the first opportunity was on his feet saying, "For 40 years I hadn't thought that I had a soul till I came here last night. Help me to find Jesus." He went forward, fell on his knees, and was so penitent it did not seem strange that that very night the publican's God sent him "to his house justified." As he met our pastor the next morning at church, he exclaimed, "Mr. Alexander, you convinced me, but Jesus saved me." It would do a stoic good to look upon his beaming face and see what grace has done for that man.

It seems to me that the most interesting feature of the AMA work in New Orleans is its leavening influence upon Roman Catholicism. I was talking after service one evening, with a beautiful girl who had been forward for prayers, and whose face wore a genuine look of deep contrition. On asking her if she attends church here regularly, she replied, "No, I go to the Catholic Church." Another girl was sitting beside a member of our family one evening when a boy behind whispered to her, "Don't you ask for prayers. If you do I'll tell the priest!" I hear that a large number in the school are professed Catholics, but are allowed to attend on account of superior instruction.

Revival in Central—English Evangelists*
—W.S. Alexander, D.D., New Orleans—
In my last letter the hope was expected that we might have good tidings to send to you. God has graciously and marvelously answered our prayer.

---

*Vol. 33 (February 1881), p. 50.

The month of November was a blessed month in Central Church.

The week of prayer in January has in other years been the beginning of real earnest revival effort. The revival seasons of blessed memory had dated from this holy week. But the coming of two English Evangelists, James Wharton and Richard Irving, during the last days of October, called for immediate action, and we decided at once to open revival meetings, and to engage in a united and earnest effort for the salvation of sinners.

While these dear brethren were resting from their voyage, the church came together and reconsecrated themselves to God. There was a quick and deep apprehension of the necessity of personal holiness and of self-denying service for Christ. Indeed, the entire month of October had been a month of prayerful preparation for the movement. Printed notices were widely distributed, and Christians went from house to house and invited people to come and seek the salvation of their souls. From the opening night the meetings were marked by deep seriousness and the evident presence of the Divine Spirit. The method of the Evangelists was simple and honest. No artificial means for exciting emotion were used. The Gospel was preached in its simplicity, its purity, and its power.

The sermons were heart-reaching, faithful and tender. The Law in its exaction and the Gospel in its provisions and promises were presented night after night. Brother Irving stayed with us ten days, and Brother Wharton three weeks. After the sermon the pastor took charge of the meetings, and called the inquirers to the "mourner's seat." Special appeals and prayers were offered. Inquirers were directed one by one how to find the Saviour, and to obtain peace in believing. At some meetings Christians were permitted and encouraged to speak of the love and preciousness of Jesus; and such a volume of testimony! We could truly say, "Lord, it is good for us to be here." As I recall the sheaves that were gathered in this glorious harvest I find much to thank God for. In two instances both the husband and the wife—all young people—were converted, and standing side by side took the vows of the Church upon them. Women who had struggled with manifold temptations, and around whom the wildest storms of sorrow had gathered, found in Christ a refuge from the storm and tempest. Young men with the hopes and possibilities of Christian manhood before them, humbly, heartily, and I believe forever, took their position as the disciples of the Son of God. When Brother Wharton was compelled to leave us to meet an engagement in another church, the pastor continued the meetings for another week, assisted by Reverend A.N. Wyckoff of the Canal Street Presbyterian Church, Reverend Dr. John Matthews, of the M.E. Church, and two able colored preachers. The fire burned brightly till the last.

The first Sabbath in December, thirty-one were received to Central Church on profession of their faith in Christ. We hope forty-eight were converted in the revival. Some joined other churches and more yet will unite themselves with us. The meetings were thronged as never before, crowds of young men attended constantly. Some of them were won for God—others were impressed—and with very many, let us hope and pray, the truth they heard will not prove to be "bread cast upon the waters," to be gathered in some future day to the glory of God.

I think I see a quickened and deepened consciousness of the right as they read it in the light of His Word, upon the part of professing Christians a painful and unyielding anxiety with those who have not submitted their hearts to God, and with many, a sincere longing to come into the fellowship of the Gospel. If this judgment be true, then how great things has the dear Lord done for us!

The Church now has 210 members. My impartial judgment is that they represent a good deal of vitality, and are beginning to realize the infinite willingness of God to bless them, and to enlarge their borders.

Central Church—New Orleans*

This Church was in 1871 the University Church and has always been intimately associated with Straight University. The president and the University are earnest workers in the Sabbath School.

From a membership of 35 in 1876, almost all of whom were old people, the membership has increased to 210. Hardly a year has

---

*Vol. 35 (September 1881), p. 273.

passed without witnessing in this church scenes of revival of interest. Every winter has had its harvest months.

The annual expenses of the Church averaging $650, are always paid promptly, and this year, in addition the church has remitted $100 to the treasury of the AMA.

Revival in Central Church and Straight University—New Orleans*
—W.S. Alexander, D.D.—

During the five weeks of continuous services 66 professed hope in the Saviour, of which number 25 were students of our university. From our family of boarding students at Stone Hall eleven were brought under conviction, who have joyously consecrated themselves to the service of the Saviour.

It was a very tender and impressive scene where among the "inquirers after God" were so many of our bright, mature students. We hope most earnestly that they all may be strong for God and for everything that is good.

On the first Sabbath in February, 31 were received to Central Church on profession of their faith, and on two succeeding Sabbaths four more, 35 in all. I mention, as a fact showing the prevalence of infant baptism, that of the 35 admitted on profession only nine received baptism, the other remaining 26 having been Christened. Our friends in the North will be glad to know that of the nearly 100 awakened and the 66 converted only six manifested any undue excitement, and but one of the number had been an attendant upon our church services. The church is stronger in every respect. The average attendance upon our Sabbath services is larger by nearly 100, and there is every indication of steady and healthful growth.

Thanksgiving at New Orleans[†]

Thanksgiving as an institution seems to be coming into more favor in this region year by year. Whether because of the source from which the Proclamation came (Abraham Lincoln) or from a better appropriation of the spirit of the day, Thanksgiving was

---

*Vol. 36 (April 1882), p. 113.
[†]Vol. 40 (January 1886), pp. 21-22.

more generally observed than usual by the churches of New Orleans.

The Central Congregational Church, of course, followed its usual custom in this respect, and joined with Straight University in the formal observance of the day. The exercise, all under the general direction of Pastor Bothwell, included, besides the customary reading of the President's Proclamation, the recitation of appropriate selections, and particularly the Proclamation of President Lincoln declaring the slaves in the seceded states free, and the last three amendments to the Constitution which naturally require a prominent place among the blessings for which these people have reason to be thankful.

Revival in New Orleans*

Thirty-three persons were received into the membership of this church on the First Sabbath in February. There were already 25 applicants for admission at our next Communion service. A few more than a hundred have given evidence of hopeful conversion since the opening of the New Year, at the meeting held at Central Church. A few persons have joined other churches because of preference but a larger number because other churches are nearer their homes. Thus the work done in this church, like the work done in the schools and colleges of the Association, accrues to the benefit of all classes of the colored people without regard to their denominational affiliations. The church itself has been greatly encouraged, and its members are hopeful of great things in the future. As indicating this fact, the festival just held to meet the insurance on the church, brought into its treasury ninety dollars.

A Young Men's Christian Association has just been organized through the efforts of the young men of Central Church, which promises to do a great and much-needed work among the young colored men of this city. Twenty-two representative young men from different churches identified themselves with this branch of the YMCA at its first meeting and many more are applicants for membership. During the month of January and the first two weeks of February, we had the efficient help of Reverend James Wharton and his wife from Furness, England.

*Vol. 40 (April 1886), pp. 103-4.

The meetings held by Messrs. Moody and Sankey were opened in this city the 9th of February. Owing to the favorable location of Central Church and its large seating capacity, and because of the interest in the meetings there, Mr. Sankey very kindly consented to sing for us three evenings during their first week in New Orleans. On Saturday evening of the same week, Mr. Moody preached to a great audience, when, on his invitation, between 50 and 60 persons came forward and kneeled as inquirers, many of whom professed their faith in a newly found Saviour before the evening's service concluded. The presence of these mighty men of God has been a great blessing to all the churches of the city. The color line had disappeared by the end of the first week, not withstanding the prudential steps of another character, taken to prevent it before the opening of the Moody meetings thus illustrating most encouragingly and beautifully that, by the "Spirit we are all baptized into one body, that in Christ there is neither Jew nor Greek, bond nor free." We believe that the prayers of the Association and the many friends of our work all over the North, who do not forget us, but generously sustain us, have been most wonderfully answered in behalf of Straight University and Central Church.

Central Congregational Church, New Orleans, La.*

—Reverend Abraham Lincoln DeMond, Pastor—

This church was organized in 1872 by a company of 32 persons. Shortly after its organization, the present house of worship— formerly a Presbyterian Church—was purchased by the AMA for $20,000. It has the largest seating capacity of any colored church in the city. During the 33 years of its history it has been a strong center of religious life among the colored people, and has also been the meeting place for large important gatherings in the interest of our people.

In this church Professor Booker T. Washington delivered his first lecture in New Orleans, being introduced by the mayor of the city. Central Church was the first church, either white or colored,

---

*Vol. 59 (October 1905), pp. 242-44.

to call a special prayer service for the city and the yellow fever epidemic, and it was in our church that the colored citizens organized the Colored Sanitary Association, which, for faithful service, has been commended by the United States Marine Hospital Service. The aim has ever been to help the people in every possible way, making it God's house and the people's church.

The young people receive special attention and our Christian Endeavor Society is becoming a strong right arm of the church. A unique and attractive feature of this work has been the training and organizing of the Christian Endeavor Orchestra by Mrs. Emma C. Harris, one of our members, who is a music teacher and who saw and seized upon the opportunity to train and use the musical talent of the young people for Christianity and the Church. The orchestra adds much to our own services and invitations are often accepted to attend other churches.

Another interesting line of our work is that of the Prison Visitation Committee, of which Mrs. M.F. Cripps is Chairman, and who has not missed a Sunday service in that work for seven years. Services are conducted in the Parish Prison every Sunday afternoon from 3 to 4 o'clock, with a sermon by the pastor, or an address by some Christian worker. In our prison song services we have had the assistance of some of the best vocal and instrumental talent in the city. Good literature is distributed among the prisoners and many of them are helpful. Clothing is also collected and given to needy ones, and there are always some who need help in that way. The best results of this work are to be seen in the changed lives of many who have been ministered to behind prison walls.

Seeking to save the sinful, teaching the young, guiding the strong, healing the sick, comforting the aged and helping the unfortunate, we are endeavoring to make this church a source of strength to all who come within the reach of its influence.

[Central Congregational Church] is conducting several features* of institutional church work. This social service work is the great need of our modern age. Our boys' club, with punchbag,

---

*Vol. 68 (January 1914), p. 590.

checkers and reading circle, has furnished wholesome amusement for the boys of our community.

Our Central Church . . . has had 46 years of worship and work,* and has a membership of 168. Not long ago it acquired the fine old house of worship of a Presbyterian church which had moved to other quarters. This large and impressive building has been changed within that it is better adapted to the needs of the congregation under Reverend H.H. Dunn. The back part of the building has been cut off from the old auditorium to make living and social rooms. The whole edifice has been put in good order by the aid of this society [Church Building Society]. The old days and the new seem to us connected in an unexpected way in this historic building whose value is over $30,000.

---

*Vol. 72 (July 1918), p. 233.

Appendix D: Membership of Congregational Churches Among Negroes in the South, 1898-1959*

Membership of Originally Congregational Churches Within the Convention of the South, 1898-1959

Year	Total Membership All Churches
1898	9,406
1907	9,541
1916	9,880
1924	9,162
1928	7,739
1938	6,135
1942	6,488
1948	5,990
1959	6,429

ALABAMA

Year	No. Churches	Membership	Largest Church	
1898	White and Negro churches not reported separately			
1907	21	1,575	Talladega 1st	237
1916	21	1,714	Talladega 1st	211
1924	19	1,142	Birmingham 1st	180
1928	15	842	Birmingham 1st	161
1938	12	730	Birmingham 1st	201
1942	11	727	Birmingham 1st	236
1948	8	635	Birmingham 1st	252
1959	9	672	Birmingham 1st	246

*Years have been selected at random.

GEORGIA

Year	No. Churches	Membership	Largest Church	
1898	68	2,516	*Atlanta 1st	397
1907	28	2,099	Atlanta 1st	600
1916	26	2,543	Atlanta 1st	955
1924	25	1,626	Atlanta 1st	500
1928	20	1,517	Atlanta 1st	479
1938	12	985	Atlanta 1st	387
1942	12	1,070	Atlanta 1st	536
1948	9	932	Atlanta 1st	453
1959	8	1,117	Atlanta 1st	600

*First Church of Atlanta has persistently been the largest Negro Congregational church in Georgia and the entire South.

KENTUCKY

Year	No. Churches	Membership	Largest Church	
1898	2	102	Louisville	70
1907	2	210	Louisville	210
1916	2	233	Louisville	174
1924	2	243	Louisville	188
1928	2	293	Louisville	202
1938	2	449	Louisville	326
1942	2	502	Louisville	357
1948	2	528	Louisville	416
1959	2	485	Louisville	391

136

LOUISIANA

Year	No. Churches	Membership	Largest Church	
1898	30	1,509	Morris Brown	203
1907	29	1,554	Jennings 1st	227
1916	16	815	Central	178
1924	18	988	Central	187
1928	17	1,027	Central	204
1938	14	955	Central	348
1942	13	1,110	Central	424
1948	13	1,190	Central	528
1959	13	1,142	Central	397

MISSISSIPPI

Year	No. Churches	Membership	Largest Church	
1898	3	—	—	—
1907	6	212	Meridian	63
1916	5	364	Tougaloo	128
1924	6	384	Tougaloo	137
1928	6	293	Tougaloo	143
1938	5	205	Caledonia	76
1942	5	157	Tougaloo	63
1948	3	133	Tougaloo	89
1959	2	*138	Tougaloo	138

---

*Meridian inactive.

137

NORTH CAROLINA

Year	No. Churches	Membership	Largest Church	
1898	42	2,087	Moncure	234
1907	57	2,659	Haywood	214
1916	50	2,427	Haywood	202
1924	55	3,445	Raleigh	505
1928	47	2,476	Raleigh	215
1938	43	1,728	Raleigh	142
1942	36	1,860	Charlotte	147
1948	38	1,865	Charlotte	125
1959	33	1,981	Charlotte	166

SOUTH CAROLINA

Year	No. Churches	Membership	Largest Church	
1898	4	—	—	—
1907	6	301	Charleston Plymouth	179
1916	11	501	Charleston Plymouth	190
1924	7	355	Charleston Plymouth	229
1928	2	239	Charleston Plymouth	209
1938	1	238	Charleston Plymouth	238
1942	2	271	Charleston Plymouth	241
1948	1	100	Charleston Plymouth	100
1950	1	133	Charleston Plymouth	133

TENNESSEE

Year	No. Churches	Membership	Largest Church	
1898	5	549	Fisk Union	214
1907	5	748	Fisk Union	259
1916	5	1,068	Fisk Union	493
1924	5	558	Chattanooga	224
1928	5	739	Chattanooga	239
1938	4	521	Memphis 2nd	179
1942	4	501	Fisk Union	164
1948	4	363	Memphis 2nd	148
1959	4	417	Memphis 2nd	174

TEXAS

Year	No. Churches	Membership	Largest Church	
1898	5	130	Paris New Hope	64
1907	6	183	Paris Rusk	56
1916	8	215	Houston	57
1924	10	421	Dallas Plymouth	107
1928	9	343	Graham Plymouth	79
1938	9	324	Corpus Christi	90
1942	9	250	Houston Pilgrim	92
1948	4	244	Houston Pilgrim	120
1959	3	244	Houston Pilgrim	226

NEW ORLEANS CHURCHES

Figures represent total number of Negro Congregationalists in New Orleans in the given years. The pattern here is not typical because of chapel membership at Old Straight University.

Year	Total Membership	Year	Total Membership
1898	556	1938	558
1907	197	1942	629
1916	342	1948	770
1924	368	1959	604
1928	537		

Appendix E: Documents

Document 1
Extracts from Letter of Chaplain Jones
Which Stimulated AMA Interest and Action
Among Freedmen*

> Camp Butler
> Newport News, Virginia
> August 21, 1861

To the Young Men's Christian Association of the City of New York

Dear Brethren:

  . . . Destitute and desperate as they are (the contrabands) they are endeavoring among themselves to keep up religious meetings on the Sabbath; and a more affecting and touching sight was scarcely ever presented to the eye of the philanthropic and benevolent Christian, than an assemblage of these poor houseless and homeless sons of Africa, stretching out their imploring hands to God, amidst the desolation of these fearful times. Their condition is one that demands the attention and sympathy of the Christian world and those who have prayed that the bands of the slave might be broken and that the oppressed might go free, can not fail to see God's hand in the work of answering their prayers, and should be ready to say, Amen—ready with the seeds of truth to enter the field and sow, that they might reap. . . .

  Let the Gospel follow in the wake of this revolution and the home bred heathen of this land will soon be beyond the needs of our sympathies. Should we not meet them with the Gospel and welcome them to its blessings as their chains drop from their hands?. . .

---

*From *American Missionary*, vol. 5 (October 1, 1861, Supplement), p. 241.

May God lead every lover of humanity to cast about him and see what his duty is, and to be on the watch, lest he should let an opportunity to become a worker together with God in these eventful times pass unnoticed and unimproved.

> Truly yours in the love of
> Christ,
> P. Franklin Jones
> Chaplain 1st Reg't N.Y.S.
> Vol.

Document 2
Letter Published by National Council of
Congregational Churches, at Which Time
$250,000 Appropriation Made to AMA—
Boston, June 1865*

. . . The whole country is now open to us. Heretofore there has been a line beyond which the Bible was restrained—a line beyond which the Gospel, full and free, regenerating human hearts and reforming human institutions, emancipating from all sin and slavery, could not go. But the resistless march of our armies has obliterated that forbidden line. Those words which are spirit and life may now be preached throughout all the land, unto all the inhabitants thereof. The Bible, as well as the black man is free: and all its great, pungent, practical truths may now be applied to every relation in life. The West was open to the friends of Christ. They entered and the result is, the salvation of our government, as well as the enlargement of the Redeemer's Kingdom. Today the South is open to the same transforming, saving truth. Shall we enter and vitalize that which is decaying and plant new churches, looking to no distant future for our "recompense of the reward"?

---

*From *American Missionary*, vol. 9 (October 1865), p. 227.

Document 3
Six Qualifications for Missionaries Among the Freedmen*

(Issued July 1866)

1. *Missionary Spirit.* As our work is to be carried on in a country devastated, and in a society demoralized, and generally made hostile by war, no one should seek, accept, or be recommended for an appointment who is not prepared to endure hardness as a good soldier of Jesus Christ—to do hard work, go to hard places, and submit, if need be to hard fare—to subordinate self to the cause and acquiesce cheerfully in the direction and supervision of those who have the matter in charge. For this, however, there can be no adequate preparation, but a true missionary spirit. None should go, then, who are influenced by either romantic or mercenary motives; who go for poetry or the pay; who wish to go South because they have failed at the North.
2. *Health.* The toil, the frequent hardships, the tax of brain and nerve, that may be encountered in the full and faithful prosecution of this work, will justify us in an appointment to no one, not enjoying good health. This is not a hygenic association, to help invalids try a change of air, or travel at others' expense.
3. *Energy.* The service demands not only vigorous work as laid out and required by others in the school room, but a disposition and ability to find something to do beyond these prescribed duties—to set oneself to work—to seek to do good for Christ and his poor, by ministering to the physical wants of the destitute; by family visitation and instruction; in Bible reading and distribution; in Sabbath school teaching and in Christian missionary labors generally.
4. *Culture and Common Sense.* It is a mistaken and mischievous idea, that "almost anybody can teach the Freedmen." Nowhere is character, in the school and out of it, more important. More than at the North, should the teacher have re-

---

*From *American Missionary*, vol. 10 (July 1866), p. 152.

sources in himself, on which he can fall back in the absence of those helps, which school laws and a correct public sentiment here afford. They only should be commissioned, least likely to make mistakes, where mistakes, when made, can so seldom be corrected.

5. *Personal Habits.* Marked singularities and idiosyncrasies of character are specifically out of place here. Moroseness or perturbance, frivolity or undue fondness of society, are too incompatible with the benevolence, gravity, and earnestness of our work, to justify the appointment, or recommendation, of any exhibiting such traits. Neither should any be commissioned who are addicted to the use of tobacco or opium, or are not pledged to total abstinence of intoxicating drinks.

6. *Experience.* As a general rule, only those should be commissioned or recommended, who have had experience teaching, and whose experience, especially as disciplinarians, has been crowned with marked success.

Document 4
Announcement 1874*

A Theological Institute free to MINISTERS OF ALL DENOMINATIONS will be held at Talladega, beginning Wednesday, December 9, and closing Thursday, December 24, [1874].

The exercises of the Institute will include lectures upon preaching and pastoral work, by leading ministers of various denominations, and by the Professors in the Theological Department of Talladega College: also of Bible studies, prayer meetings, and exercises in preaching. All ministers attending will receive free entertainment among the citizens of Talladega; but the gathering is likely to be so large that those who intend to come should send their names before hand, if possible. Reduced fares on the railroads will be applied for.

---

*From *American Missionary*, vol. 18 (December 1874), p. 275.

Document 5
Talladega Seminary Curriculum, 1910*

A. *Bible Training Course:* To aid those whose preparatory work is deficient and who . . . are not able to take . . . the more advanced course.
B. *Classical Course:* A curriculum which compares favorably with that of the older seminaries in the North granting the Bachelor of Divinity Degree.
C. *English Course:* Granting Diploma
D. *Correspondence Course*

---

*From *American Missionary*, vol. 63 (December 1910), p. 609.

Document 6
Seminary Curriculum, 1926*
Talladega Theological Seminary
1872—1926

Faculty and Instructors
Rev. Frederick A. Sumner, A.M., President

Rev. James Hyslop, A.M., Ph.D., Dean
      Professor of Homiletics and Church History

Rev. Charles Arthur Jaquith, B.D., A.M.
      Professor of Biblical History and Literature

Rev. Arnold E. Gregory, B.D.
      Professor of Theology and New Testament

Prof. Albert Sidney Kilbourn, A.B.
      Professor of Applied Sociology and Rural Economics

---

*From a brochure published by Talladega College in 1926.

Prof. Tourgee A. DeBose, Mus. B.
Instructor in Voice Culture and Church Music

James T. Cater, A.M.
Instructor in Education and Psychology

Maintenance and Relation to Talladega College

Talladega Theological Seminary is the one Theological Seminary maintained by the A.M.A. for the training of Negro Ministers. It is a co-ordinate department of Talladega College, and by a system of cross credits, students credits, students can take college and seminary degrees in six years. Similar work in the colleges of the same rank as Talladega is accepted in the Seminary.

Aims

The Seminary stands for character, scholarship, and service. It aims to develop leadership for the race, through efficient training under competent guidance.

Course of Study

The Seminary maintains two courses of study—the Theological and the Diploma. Courses are also offered in Social Service Practice, Community Methods, Rural Economics, Music, Religious Education and Sunday School work.

The College and Seminary offer courses in the Bible, Christian Doctrine, Social Service, Church History, and the History of Religions, looking toward Y.M.C.A., Y.W.C.A., and other forms of Christian Service.

Requirements for Admission and Graduation

For the Theological Course, the four years of College are desirable. As this is not in all cases feasible, men having two years of college work are accepted. Upon completion of the course the degree of B.D. is given. Two years of Greek are offered to all who have had two years of preparatory Greek. For admission to the Diploma Course, the completion of the High School Course, or its equivalent, is required. On completion of the High School course, a Diploma will be awarded. Every student possible will be encouraged to prepare for and take the B.D. course.

Equipment and General Advantages

The Seminary is housed in a commodious building, equipped with steam heat, electric lights and shower baths. Students have the advantage of the college and Seminary libraries, of college classes, and student societies. All denominations are received on equal terms.

Expenses

Students pay for tuition, board, laundry and incidental fees. The bare necessities are not less than $200 a year. There are opportunities for self-help, and some student funds are available under certain conditions for those whose scholarship is satisfactory.

For further information address James Hyslop, Dean
394 W. Battle Street
Talladega, Alabama

Document 7
A Typical Account of the Origin and Early Development of a Congregational Church Among Negroes in the South*

Congregationalism in Chattanooga
—Reverend Joseph E. Smith—

Very early in November, 1866, Reverend E.D. Tade, his wife and sister, were sent by the American Missionary Association and the Freedman's Aid Commission to Chattanooga to take charge of the colored schools in Chattanooga. For the first few months the mission labors were distributed among all the churches and places of worship for the colored people. But this scattered effort was soon thought to be unwise. A prayer meeting was first established and in the school room and then followed preaching, first in the morning and later in the evening. The congregations were large and attentive. But as the various churches

---

*From *American Missionary*, vol. 51 (September 1897), pp. 236-37.

got in order and in places of their own, both the Sunday school and congregation gradually reduced in members.

At the close of the school early in June, 1867, and as the missionary and teachers were preparing to go to their homes in the North, a number of young men called upon the missionary and said, "What shall we do for Sunday-school and preaching when you go away?" As several of these young men had recently professed loyalty and love to Christ, they proposed to form themselves into a church if the Reverend Mr. Tade would only remain and preach to them. After much prayer and consultation Mr. Tade decided to remain, and on the 9th of June, 1867 The First Congregational Church at Chattanooga, Tennessee, was organized with sixteen members. Under the six years' regular pastorate of Mr. Tade, the little church increased in influence and usefulness, and in numbers to 77. The six years of smooth regularity and growth under Mr. Tade's pastorate were followed by six years of changes and disappointments which greatly discouraged and scattered the flock.

Just at this time of struggle when the church was without a pastor, three visitors in their turn came to our city—cholera, yellow fever and smallpox. The mission of these visitors seemed to be . . . to break up the Congregational Church. These three dreadful diseases swept away a large number of our people. About the same time came another visitor though of a very different character from that just mentioned. But its influence was almost as harmful to our church as the other. This was the assembling of a large conference of one of the old time churches of the South. They told the members of our church that they knew nothing about Congregational churches; that their mothers and fathers, their grandfathers and grandmothers knew nothing about such a church; that it was a new thing never heard of until the war; and that it was not a church but a government society; that the founder was sent by the government and not by God; that they teach a book religion and do not believe in travails; and that because it was not a true church no minister would stay with them, and that the whole thing must fail soon, and every Negro who had any race pride would join one of the old regular churches. These methods and many others which prevailed in those days and are not powerless yet, were diligently used against the little church, and many went away and walked with us no more.

These trials shook the faith of some who remained and put doubts in the minds of others about the future life of the church. It was this discouraged feeling born of doubt and uncertainty, on the part of the church itself about its own future life, that the present pastor had to meet, and of all the obstacles, was the most difficult to overcome. This time the church was doing nothing toward self-support. The American Missionary Association was paying all the bills. When, finally, the church itself believed that it had come to stay, and that it had a promising future, the members came together with a new courage born of a new faith and soon won a way to recognition from other denominations. They at once began the work of self-help, taking more and more of the burden each year; until seven years ago they raised the flag of entire self-support, and our mother, the AMA, who stood faithfully by us through all our trials and encouraged us with substantial aid, gave us an honorable dismission and her benediction. . . .

Document 8
Early Conflict with Other Denominations*
1862

From: Fortress Monroe, Virginia

Mr. Lockwood wrote us under date February 15, that a missionary from another Board (Baptist), had been there the previous Sabbath; a man whom we judge to be entirely unfit to meet the wants of the people.

He had been (he says) an overseer on a plantation at the South and though he professed to not like slavery, he retained all the prejudices of slavery against the colored race. I am surprised that

---

*From *American Missionary* (1862).

the Board could not better appreciate the spirit of this people, than to think of such a man as a fit delegate to them, because he had acted as a slaveholder's preacher.

As soon as he arrived, he went round among the Authorities at the Fort, trying to poison their minds against our mission, and even attempted the same thing among the colored people. On Saturday he went over to some of the brethren near Hampton. There he told Brother Herbert that the colored people were becoming saucy under our treatment, and that those who eat and sleep with them were not their friends. Mrs. Shepard, the colored woman who boards Brother Herbert and Hardcastle, prepared him (the Baptist preacher) a turkey dinner, but he would not stay to eat it.

Sabbath morning he came out and I went over with him. He said on the way, that he would not, on any consideration, eat with colored people, or in any way put himself on a level with them. He told me plainly, that the manner of H. and others, showed that the people were becoming spoiled, and he requested that I not introduce him as brother, and have a general shaking of the hands for he did not like it. As in courtesy bound I requested him to open the meeting, read a chapter, and make a few remarks but like the animal in the fable, once allowed to get his head in, he had no trouble in getting in his shoulders, and his whole body. He occupied the whole time in a sermon of about usual length, prayed, sung a hymn, and closed the meeting, and requested the members of the Baptist Church to tarry for a church meeting. I and the teachers thought it was our privilege to tarry. He remarked that he had noticed that the people were becoming independent. Brother Herbert remarked in reply, that he was sorry that any independence that might be noticed in a few, should be thrown upon the whole. He asked them if they would like to leave here; they said they would, if they could take their friends with them now in secessiondom: but at the present, they thought it best to bide their time, rather than go to the West Indies, as he proposed. He then argued the point of their remaining strict Baptist, and proposed that they should decide whether they desired a pastor to be sent.

Soon afterwards he left. I then suggested that the people consider the matter, and decide next Sabbath; remarking that I had told him that our Board (AMA) would doubtless have no objection to a strict Baptist missionary, provided he could labor cordially in conjunction with us, but he had told me that they must have the whole control over church matters, or none. Deacon Thompson Walker spoke for the rest, and said they were to decide at once to cling to our mission. There was an unanimous vote accordingly. And next evening and the next, they confirmed the matter with joyous unanimity. We had enough, said they, of proslavery ministers. . . . The Lord direct in this peculiar exigency.

Document 9
Provisions of Agreement for the American
Missionary Association to Be an Agent of the
Board of Home Missions of Congregational
Christian Churches*

The American Missionary Association was included as a constituent division of the Board of Home Missions which was organized in 1937. For many years the Congregational churches had been supporting a number of other home missionary societies. These were the Congregational Church Building Society, the Congregational Sunday School Extension Society, the Congregational Board of Ministerial Relief, the Congregational Education Society, and the Congregational Publishing Society, familiarly known as the Pilgrim Press. It was felt that if these societies were united, greater simplicity in promotion would follow, to the benefit of all concerned. The separate societies retained their corporate existence under their own charters. In transferring Missions, each society entered into contractual agreements with the Board

---

*Minutes of a Special Meeting of the Excutive Committee, the American Missionary Association, April 5, 1937. Fred L. Brownlee, *New Day Ascending* (Boston: Pilgrim Press, 1946), pp. 263-64.

relative to its properties, trust funds, endowments, and the essential character of its work. The American Missionary Association's agreement contains the following provisions:—

Resolved, that the Board of Home Missions of the Congregational and Christian Churches be and hereby is authorized and empowered to proceed as an agent of this Association to conduct and carry on its obligations and operations, and as such representative and agent the said corporation shall receive and direct the use of all income and funds relating to obligations and operation so taken over, which are now in or may hereafter come into the treasury of this Association, or to which it may be now or hereafter be entitled, and be it further

Resolved, that the basic condition of this grant of agency shall be the agreement by the Board of Home Missions of the Congregational and Christian Churches to use all of the income and funds, and any of the property of the American Missionary Association utilized in the carrying out of the Association's activities in accordance with its charter provisions, and in such use to recognize the circumstances surrounding the history of the work and the origin of these funds and harmony with the wishes of their donors and the spirit and tradition of this Association, particularly in keeping with the Association's work for the welfare and education of the members of the Negro race. . . .

Notes

Preface

1. One of the exceptions to this limitation of Black theology is Gayraud Wilmore's *Black Religion and Black Radicalism* (Garden City, N.Y.: Doubleday, 1973).
2. H. Richard Niebuhr, *The Kingdom of God in America* (Chicago: Willet, Clark & Co., 1937), pp. ix-x.

Chapter 1: "The Pregnant Source of a New Aggression"

1. H. Richard Niebuhr, *The Kingdom of God in America* (Chicago: Willet, Clark & Co., 1937), p. 198.
2. H. Richard Niebuhr, *The Social Sources of Denominationalism* (New York: Henry Holt and Co., 1929), p. 89.
3. Ibid., pp. 89-90.
4. Ernst Troeltsch, *Soziallehren der Christlichen Kircher und Gruppen*, p. 27; quoted and translated in Niebuhr, *The Social Sources of Denominationalism*, op. cit., p. 29. The English translation by Olive Wyon reads: "It is the lower classes which do the really creative work, forming communities on a genuine religious basis. They alone unite imagination and simplicity of feeling with a non-reflective habit of mind, a primitive energy, and an urgent sense of need. On such a foundation alone is it possible to build up an unconditional authoritative faith in a Divine Revelation with simplicity of surrender and unshaken certainty. Only within a fellowship of this kind is there room for those who have a sense of spiritual need, and who have not acquired the habit of intellectual reasoning, which always regards everything from a relative point of view. All great religious movements based on Divine revelation which have created large communities have always issued from circles of this kind. The meaning and capacity for development of the religious movement which arose in this way were always dependent upon the power and depth of the stimulus which had been imparted by such a naïve revelation, and, on the other hand, upon the energy of the religious conviction which gave to this stimulus a divine and absolute authority." (Ernst Troeltsch, *The Social Teaching of the Christian Churches*, trans. Olive Wyon [New York: Macmillan, 1931], p. 44.)
5. Ibid., p. 27.
6. See ibid., p. 90.
7. Report of the Sixteenth Annual Meeting of the American Missionary Association, Oberlin, Ohio, 1862; quoted in Wesley A. Hotchkiss, *A Door So Wide* (Centennial Series; New York: American Missionary Association, 1965), No. 1, pp. 3-4.
8. Paraphrased from General Association of New York, 1863 and addressed to AMA; quoted in Hotchkiss, *A Door So Wide*, op. cit., p. 5.
9. See Niebuhr, *The Kingdom of God in America*, op. cit., p. 198.

Chapter 2: "An Old Spirit in New Form"

1. Douglas Horton, *Congregationalism: A Study in Church Polity* (London: Independent Press, 1952), p. 9.
2. Karl Barth, *Dogmatics in Outline* (New York: Harper and Bros., 1959), p. 141.
3. See Rudolf Bultmann, *Theology of the New Testament*, vol. 1 (New York: Charles Scribner's Sons, 1951), pp. 192-203.
4. See Deuteronomy at the giving of the Law, 1 Kings 8:14ff.
5. Acts 5:11; 8:1, 3.
6. Acts 2:37-41.
7. Singular—Earlier chapters applied to the local congregation at Jerusalem: Acts 11:26; 13:1; 14:27; and 15:3 applied to Antioch and Syria; 18:22 to Caesarea; and 20:17 to Ephesus. Plural—15:41; 16:5, etc.
8. Singular—The church in a particular city: Rom. 16:1; 1 Cor. 1:2; Col. 4:16; 1 Thess. 1:1; 2 Thess. 1:1; of house churches: 1 Cor.16:19; Col. 4:15, etc. Plural—Churches of various places: 2 Cor. 8:1; Gal. 1:22; 1 Thess. 2:14; all churches of Christ: Rom. 16:16; 1 Cor. 7:17, etc.
9. 1 Cor. 11:18; 14:19, 23, 28, 34, 35.
10. 1 Cor. 1:2; 2 Cor. 1:1.
11. Rom. 16:16; Gal. 1:22; 1 Thess. 2:14.
12. See Alan Richardson, *A Theological Word Book of the Bible* (New York: Macmillan, 1950), pp. 46-48, for additional development of the biblical idea of the church.
13. Claude Welch, *The Reality of the Church* (New York: Charles Scribner's Sons, 1958), pp. 152-64.
14. Rom. 8:1; 9:1; 16:3, 12; etc.
15. *The Gospel, the Church and Society: Congregationalism Today* (New York: General Council of Congregational Christian Churches, 1938), p. 8.
16. Ibid., p. 9.
17. Ibid.
18. Ibid., p. 10.
19. Daniel Jenkins, *Congregationalism: A Restatement* (London: Faber and Faber, 1954), p. 33.
20. Horton, *Congregationalism*, op. cit., p. 10.
21. *The Gospel, the Church and Society*, op. cit., p. 10.
22. Ibid.
23. Ibid., p. 102.
24. Ibid., p. 182.
25. Ibid., pp. 183-84.
26. Walter Marshall Horton, in *The Nature of the Church*, ed. R. Newton Flew (New York: Harper and Bros., 1951), p. 278.
27. *The Gospel, the Church and Society*, op. cit., p. 183.
28. See ibid., p. 185.
29. Ibid., p. 20.
30. Ibid.

Chapter 3: "The Time Has Come"

1. Clifton E. Olmstead, *History of Religion in the United States* (Englewood Cliffs, N.J.: Prentice-Hall, 1960), pp. 81-82.
2. The best and largest collection of original documents relating to the *Amistad* incident is in the Amistad Research Center at Dillard University, New Orleans, La. The Amistad story may also be found in the court records and other data on file in the Sterling Library of Yale University, and in writings based thereon; in letters to the American Missionary Association from Sherad Soule and from the registrars of Fisk University, Chicago Theological Seminary, and Yale Divinity School; and in a paper written by Roland H. Bainton of the Yale University Divinity School. See Fred L. Brownlee, *New Day Ascending* (Boston: Pilgrim Press, 1946), p. 7.
3. Dwight O.W. Holmes, *The Evolution of the Negro College* (New York: Teachers College, Columbia University, 1934), p. 76.
4. *American Missionary*, vol. 9, p. 201.
5. Ibid., vol. 60, p. 300.
6. Ibid., vol. 12 (May 1868), p. 99.
7. Ibid., vol. 5 (October 1861), p. 24. (Supplement issued immediately after the outbreak of the Civil War.)
8. Ibid. See Document 1 for extracts from Chaplain Jones's letter.
9. *American Missionary*, vol. 5 (October 1861), p. 242.
10. Ibid.
11. Ibid.
12. See ibid.
13. See Appendix A, Table I.
14. *American Missionary*, vol. 60 (December 1906), p. 300. Note that the total expenditures for the AMA in 1864 were $96,305.30. The amount of $55,788.41, or more than 60 percent, was spent for the Freedmen. The second largest expenditure, $9,685.70, went to the Mendi Mission in Sierra Leone, West Africa. It was also estimated that about $5,000 in books, clothes, and other commodities were given to Freedmen of the slave states. These and other figures illustrate that AMA attention and support was directed more and more to the South and that its work on other fields decreased.
15. Ibid., vol. 18 (August 1874), p. 184.
16. Ibid.
17. Ibid., vol. 8 (August 1864), p. 186.
18. Ibid. See also Appendix B for a partial listing of associations that voted support and for sample resolutions.
19. *American Missionary*, vol. 79 (June 1925), p. 105.
20. See Document 2, "Letter Published by National Council of Congregational Churches," June 1865, when a $250,000 appropriation was made to the AMA. The letter is a council statement on the church's mission to Freedmen.
21. See Chapter 9.
22. See *American Missionary*, vol. 12 (May 1868), p. 100.
23. Ibid., vol. 32 (April 1878), p. 99.

24. See James M. Gustafson, *Treasure in Earthen Vessels: The Church as a Human Community* (New York: Harper and Bros., 1961), pp. 111-12.
25. See Gerhard Lenski, *The Religious Factor: A Sociological Study of Religion's Impact on Politics, Economics, and Family Life* (Garden City, N.Y.: Doubleday, 1961), p. 303.
26. In ibid. Lenski observes that "the subculture of every socio-religious group is always profoundly affected by the social situation of the group. The social situation provides, in Toynbee's terms, the challenges to which the group must respond: it provides the problems to which solutions must be found."

Chapter 4: "Awaiting New Wonders"

1. See Appendix A, Tables II and III.
2. In his *Black Religion and Black Radicalism* (Garden City, N.Y.: Doubleday, 1973), pp. 1-2, Gayraud Wilmore confirms this idea. He writes: "The religion of the descendants of the Africans who were brought to the Western world as slaves has, from the very beginning, been something less and something more than what is generally regarded as the Christian religion. It could not have been otherwise. The religious beliefs and rituals of any people are inevitably and inseparably bound up with the material and psychological realities of their daily existence. Certainly those realities for the slaves were vastly different from those experienced by the slavemasters. In a way, the slavemasters understood this better than the missionaries and were never so sanguine as the latter about the possibilities of master and slave sharing the same religion."
3. H. Richard Niebuhr, *The Kingdom of God in America* (Chicago: Willet, Clark & Co., 1937), pp. 30-31.
4. We suggest two sources that give adequate treatments using this approach: Benjamin E. Mays and Joseph William Nicholson, *The Negro's Church* (New York: Institute of Social and Religious Research, 1933), esp. chaps. 1 and 2; and Carter G. Woodson, *The History of the Negro Church*, 2d ed. (New York: Associated Publishers, 1921).
5. With the possible exception of Negro spirituals, folklore, and prayer and sermon clichés that have stood the test of time, frequent use, and the patience of God.
6. W.E.B. DuBois, *The Souls of Black Folk* (New York: A.C. McClurg and Co., 1903), p. 144.
7. Ibid.
8. Ibid.
9. Ibid., p. 145.
10. Alfred Métraux, *Voodoo in Haiti*, trans. Hugo Charteris (New York: Schocken Books, 1972), p. 15.
11. Again Wilmore's *Black Religion and Black Radicalism*, op. cit., pp. 10-11, is helpful here: "The slave made an adaptation to Christianity that rendered it something more than a dispassionate system of belief and a code of pious behavior. He did accept the spirited, revivalistic interpretation of the impassioned Methodist and Baptist missionaries and imitated them, but he also

went far beyond their understanding of Christianity to fashion it to his own social and recreational, as well as personal, spiritual needs.

"One of the outstanding white missionaries in the South during the first part of the 19th century was . . . the Reverend Charles Colcock Jones. . . . Jones complained of perversions of the Gospel among the newly converted slaves and was particularly exercised over their propensity to antinomianism, the belief that the moral law is of no effect to one who has come under the dispensation of the Gospel. Jones observed about the religious practices he witnessed: 'True religion they are inclined to place in profession, in forms and ordinances, and in excited states of feeling and true confession, in dreams, visions, trances, voices—all bearing a perfect or striking resemblance to some form or type which has been handed down for generations, or which has been originated in the wild fancy of some religious teacher among them. (Charles C. Jones, *The Religious Instruction of Negroes in the United States* [Savannah: T. Purse Co., 1842], pp. 125ff.)

"Jones describes the slave's concept of the Supreme Being and of the Person of Christ as indefinite and conquered. It is interesting to note, in this connection, that the spirituals rarely express Christological interest, nor is their subject matter particularly theistic in emphasis. As far as Christ is concerned, some of the slaves had heard of someone by that name, but did not know who he was or were inclined, said Jones, to identify him with Mohammed, the prophet of Islam. (This is not to suggest, however, that all or even most of the slaves had any previous acquaintance with Islam.)

"The Mohammedan Africans remaining of the old stock of importations, although accustomed to hear the Gospel preached, have been known to accommodate Christianity to Mohammedanism. 'God', say they, 'is Allah, and Jesus is Mohammed—the religion is the same, but different countries have different names' (Jones, ibid.).

"It was reported that in Georgia some slaves had a religion based on their own experiences, the experience of God with them, and upon various visions and revelations. Even though 'churched Negroes' respected the Bible and learned to read it before they could read anything else, among many slaves there was a contempt for 'book religion,' not merely because they had to depend upon oral instruction, but because they possessed great self-esteem and confidence in their own manner of believing and worshipping God. For them, 'The Spirit within' was superior to the Bible as a guide to religious knowledge. . . . "

12. DuBois, *The Souls of Black Folk*, op. cit., p. 147.
13. Paul Radin, ed., *God Struck Me Dead: Religious Conversion Experiences and Autobiographies of Negro Ex-Slaves* (Nashville: Social Science Institute, Fisk University, 1945), p. ix.
14. DuBois, *The Souls of Black Folk*, op. cit., pp. 147-48.
15. Paul Radin, ed., *God Struck Me Dead*, op. cit., pp. vi-vii, explains the conversion experience of the newly emancipated in more psychological terms: "[In the conversion experience the Black person] . . . found a fixed point and he needed a fixed point for both within and outside of himself, he

could see only vacillation and endless shifting. . . . It would not have been enough to fool oneself. They had to convince themselves under conditions that were always more than likely to give the lie. So they had definitely to be struck down; conversion had to be in the nature of a stroke of lightning which would enter at the top of their head and emerge from their toes. They had to meet God, be baptized by him in the river of Jordan personally, become identified with him. . . .

"So here at last, in . . . the natural striving for a unified personality, for a fixed God as the center of the world who would demand a non-recalcitrant obedience and faith, a new world was forged. Small wonder then that he who achieved it could only visualize it as a rebirth or that he could picture it as attainable only after many dangers had been overcome, after one had been literally suspended over the very brinks of hell."

Chapter 5: "Broad and Deep Foundations"

1. *American Missionary*, vol. 1 (October 1896), p. 3.
2. Wesley A. Hotchkiss, "Congregationalists and Negro Education," *The Journal of Negro Education*, Summer 1960, p. 289.
3. Quoted by Hotchkiss, ibid., pp. 289-90.
4. Ibid.
5. Wesley A. Hotchkiss, *A Door So Wide* (Centennial Series; New York: AMA, 1965), No.1, p. 5.
6. "These people were called 'Contrabands' because they were considered by the Union Army to be in the same category with other captured enemy supplies and valuables" (ibid.).
7. See Appendix A, Table IV, for the location and number of schools in 1871.
8. See Appendix A, Table V.
9. See Appendix A, Table VI.
10. Hotchkiss, "Congregationalists and Negro Education," op. cit., p. 291.
11. Augustus Field Beard, *A Crusade of Brotherhood* (Boston: Pilgrim Press, 1909), p. 117.
12. Hotchkiss, "Congregationalists and Negro Education," op. cit., p. 292.
13. *American Missionary*, vol. 8 (November 1864), p. 262.
14. See Document 3.
15. John G. Fee, *Autobiography* (Chicago: National Christian Association, 1891), p. 15.
16. Beard, *A Crusade of Brotherhood*, op. cit., p. 150.
17. Ibid., p. 139.
18. See Appendix A, Table IV.
19. Hotchkiss, "Congregationalists and Negro Education," op. cit., p. 292; see Beard, *A Crusade of Brotherhood*, op. cit., p. 147.
20. Hotchkiss, "Congregationalists and Negro Education," op. cit., p. 292.
21. W.E.B. DuBois, *The Souls of Black Folk* (New York: A.C. McClurg and Co., 1903), p. 100. DuBois was a graduate of Fisk University and an able product of the AMA.

Chapter 6: "A Controlling Power in a Dark Land"

1. *American Missionary*, vol. 19 (June 1875), p. 124.
2. See Chapter 5.
3. *American Missionary*, vol. 14 (July 1870), p. 160.
4. Ibid.
5. *American Missionary*, vol. 10 (July 1866), p. 155.
6. Ibid., p. 156.
7. Ibid.
8. Ibid., vol. 9 (November 1865), p. 251.
9. Ibid., vol. 10 (July 1866), p. 156.
10. *The Congregationalist*, May 1868, p. 3.
11. Ibid.
12. Ibid., p. 4.
13. Ibid.
14. *American Missionary*, vol. 13 (December 1869), p. 270.
15. Ibid., vol. 14 (July 1870), p. 160.
16. Ibid.
17. Ibid.
18. Ibid., pp. 160-61.

Chapter 7: "Indulging a Christian Hope"

1. Augustus Field Beard, *A Crusade of Brotherhood* (Boston: Pilgrim Press, 1909), p. 199.
2. *American Missionary*, vol. 7 (July 1863), p. 156. The letter was preceded by this editorial comment: "The following stirring extract is from the private letter of an honored servant of God in the West. We wish every Christian in our country had as true a realization of our tremendous responsibility. We should then see a gathering up, and putting forth of the energies of the church, such as the world has never yet known."
3. Ibid., vol. 8 (August 1864), p. 194.
4. Ibid., July 1864, p. 180.
5. Ibid., vol. 13 (December 1869), p. 270.
6. Ibid., vol. 19 (May 1875), p. 98.
7. Ibid.
8. Ibid.
9. Ibid., vol. 19 (September 1875), p. 195.
10. H. Richard Niebuhr, *The Social Sources of Denominationalism* (New York: Henry Holt and Co., 1929), p. 262.
11. *American Missionary*, vol. 14 (July 1870), p. 147.
12. Ibid., vol. 14 (March 1870), pp. 58-59.
13. Ibid., vol. 16 (December 1872), p. 279.
14. Ibid., vol. 14 (May 1870), p. 99.
15. See ibid., vol. 16 (December 1872), p. 279.
16. Benjamin E. Mays and Joseph William Nicholson, *The Negro's Church* (New York: Institute of Social and Religious Research, 1933), p. 40.

17. Ibid.
18. As early as 1868 a church had been organized at Talladega, Alabama and "instruction in preaching" was advertised and given under the auspices of the missionary church. This may well have been the first rudimentary seminary for Negroes in the South. At any rate, the college was the first institution of higher learning for the Freedman in the state of Alabama.
19. *American Missionary*, vol. 13 (March 1869), p. 63.
20. Ibid., vol. 15 (June 1871), p. 132.
21. See Document 4.
22. *American Missionary*, vol. 32 (April 1878), p. 111.
23. Ibid., vol. 14 (February 1875), p. 29.
24. Ibid., vol. 53 (July 1899), p. 55.
25. See ibid., vol. 40 (February 1886), p. 33.
26. See *The Congregationalist*, May 1868.
27. *American Missionary*, vol. 33 (March 1881), pp. 67-68.
28. See Appendix B, Table VIII.

Chapter 8: "That the Circumference of These Span"

1. E. Franklin Frazier, *Black Bourgeoisie* (Chicago: Free Press, 1957), p. 20.
2. Augustus Field Beard, *A Crusade of Brotherhood* (Boston: Pilgrim Press, 1909), p. 168.
3. As late as 1945, Drake and Cayton found that "members of the Congregational church (in Chicago) were keenly aware of the class position which it occupied, and were sensitive to criticisms of its alleged exclusiveness. One member said: 'I so often hear nasty remarks about the membership. They will say that it is not a church for black folk; that they don't want you here unless you are nearly white, so it is no use to try to join the church for you are not welcome. Now, not a word of that is true, for if you will go there you will find members of all colors. It just has the name of being a blue vein church.' While none of these 'upper' churches are 'blue vein,' they do perhaps have a higher proportion of light members than other churches." (St. Clair Drake and Horace R. Cayton, *Black Metropolis: A Study of Negro Life in a Northern City* [New York: Harcourt, Brace and Co., 1945], p. 539.)
4. *American Missionary*, vol. 45 (October 1891), p. 353.
5. Beard, *A Crusade of Brotherhood*, op. cit., p. 230.
6. Ibid.
7. Ibid. "Companionship" means literally "the sharing of the bread." Within the context of the Christian church—its faith and belief—"sympathetic companionship," or "selective sharing of the bread," could quite well be the equivalent of the "the fencing of the table." For the AMA, then, "sympathetic sharing of the bread" or "the fencing of the table" and the common life of the church was based on the idea that only the "regenerate" were worthy to commune. Unfortunately, the "regenerate" and the upper echelon happened to be the same. One cannot conclude, however, that only the "regenerate" or the "elite" were communicants of the Negro Congregational churches. Since there was no central control, no rigid means of inspection or selectivity, owing to the "reasonable" autonomy of each local

church, "selective companionship" could not be enforced. Sinner and saint, rich and poor, illiterate and enlightened crept in and shared the common loaf.

8. Ibid.
9. Ibid.
10. See Appendix A, Table IX. By the end of 1925 the total number of graduates had risen to 10,000. "Between 1926 and 1931 inclusive, a period of six years, 9,257 Negro men and women received college degrees from American institutions. In other words, approximately four times as many Negroes were graduated from colleges between 1909 and 1931, a period of twenty-two years, as in the eighty-nine years previous to 1909. In 1930 and 1931, 4,051 Negro students were graduated from college, which is more than the number graduated in the eighty-nine years between 1820 and 1909." (Benjamin E. Mays and Joseph William Nicholson, *The Negro's Church* [New York: Institute of Social and Religious Research, 1933], pp. 49-50.)
11. See Charles S. Johnson, *Encyclopedia Americana* (New York: Americana Corporation, 1960), vol. 20, p. 271.
12. Ibid.
13. See Appendix A, Tables X and XI.
14. See Howard W. Odum, *Man's Quest for Social Guidance* (New York: Henry Holt and Co., 1927), p. 189.
15. John Hope Franklin, *From Slavery to Freedom* (New York: Knopf, 1948), pp. 428-29.
16. Ibid.
17. Mays and Nicholson, *The Negro's Church*, op. cit., p. 95.
18. "There was an increase of 73.3 percent for Norfolk, 41.7 percent for Jacksonville, and 34.3 for Birmingham. Mr. Work in 'The Race Problem in Cross Section,' in the January 1924 issue of *Social Forces*, reports that the increase of Negro urban population in the South from 1910 to 1920 was 66,000 more than the increase, for the same period, in the number of Negroes who went North from the South" (Odum, *Man's Quest for Social Guidance*, op. cit., p. 188). In 1920 there were many southern cities in which a third of the population was Black. Among these, Charleston had 47.5 percent; Savannah, 47.1; Montgomery, 45.6; Jacksonville, 45.5; Macon, 43.6; Augusta, 43.0; Birmingham and Mobile, 39.3; and Memphis, 37.7.
19. Only eight of these churches were connected with preexisting schools. One hundred seventeen were in other communities.
20. *American Missionary*, vol. 56 (January 1902), p. 24.
21. Ibid. See *Survey*, vol. 70 (January 1916), p. 586.
22. *American Missionary*, vol. 67 (December 1913), p. 546.
23. Ibid.
24. Ibid., vol. 56 (January 1902), p. 40.
25. Ibid., May 1902, pp. 250ff.
26. Ibid.
27. Ibid.
28. Ibid., vol. 64 (December 1911), p. 220.
29. Ibid., December 1910, p. 606.
30. Ibid., vol. 65 (July 1911), p. 33.

Chapter 9: "The Marking of Time, a Faint Whimper, and Confused Deliberations"

1. James M. Gustafson, *Treasure in Earthen Vessels: The Church as a Human Community* (New York: Harper and Bros., 1961), p. 35.
2. Ibid., pp. 34-35.
3. Ibid., p. 36.
4. John G. Fee, an AMA teacher in the South, "withdrew from the American Missionary Association because he believed the Association had become sectarian, when in 1865, it was adopted by the National Council of Congregational Churches as its agent in freedmen's welfare" (Fred L. Brownlee, *New Day Ascending* [Boston: Pilgrim Press, 1946], p. 97).
5. "Increasing use is being made of denominational machinery" (*66th Annual Report*, AMA, 1911-1912).
6. Ibid., pp. 261ff.
7. Ibid.
8. *67th Annual Report*, AMA, 1913.
9. Ibid.
10. Ibid.
11. Ibid.

Chapter 10: "Decreasing Demands for Checks from Dad"

1. See Appendix A, Table XVI.
2. See *American Missionary*, vol. 76 (December 1922), p. 464.
3. See Appendix A, Tables XVII, XVIII, XIX, and XX.
4. *The Negro Year Book* (Tuskegee Institute, Ala.: Negro Year Book Co., 1921-22), p. 236.
5. *American Missionary*, vol. 75 (June 1921), pp. 93-94.
6. *79th Annual Report*, AMA, 1925.
7. H. Richard Niebuhr, *The Kingdom of God in America* (Chicago: Willet, Clark & Co., 1937), p. 177.

Chapter 11: "The Children Is Crying"

1. H. Richard Niebuhr, *The Kingdom of God in America* (Chicago: Willet, Clark & Co., 1937), p. 198.

Bibliography

The American Missionary, 1859-1926.

Annual Report: American Missionary Association.

Barth, Karl. *Dogmatics in Outline.* New York: Harper and Bros., 1959.

Beard, Augustus Field. *A Crusade of Brotherhood: A History of the American Missionary Association.* Boston: Pilgrim Press, 1909.

Berger, Peter L. *The Noise of Solemn Assemblies.* Garden City, N.Y.: Doubleday, 1961.

Bonhoeffer, Dietrich. *Life Together.* New York: Harper and Bros., 1954.

Brown, F.J., and Roucek, J.S., eds. *One America.* 3d ed. New York: Prentice-Hall, 1952.

Brownlee, Fred L. *New Day Ascending.* Boston: Pilgrim Press, 1946.

Bultmann, Rudolf. *Theology of the New Testament.* Vol. 1. New York: Charles Scribner's Sons, 1951.

Clark, Elmer T. *Small Sects in America.* Rev. ed. Nashville: Abingdon-Cokesbury, 1949.

Cogley, John, ed. *Religion in America.* New York: Meridian Books, 1958.

Dale, R.W. *History of English Congregationalism.* Book I. London, 1907.

Drake, St. Clair, and Cayton, Horace R. *Black Metropolis: A Study of Negro Life in a Northern City.* New York: Harcourt, Brace and Co., 1945.

DuBois, W.E.B. *The Souls of Black Folk.* New York: A.C. McClurg and Co., 1903.

Fee, John G. *Autobiography.* Chicago: National Christian Association, 1891.

Flew, R. Newton, ed. *The Nature of the Church.* New York: Harper and Bros., 1951.

Frazier, Edward Franklin. *Black Bourgeoisie.* Chicago: Free Press, 1957.

————. *The Negro Church in America.* New York: Schocken Books, 1964.

Franklin, John Hope. *From Slavery to Freedom: A History of American Negroes.* New York: Alfred A. Knopf, 1948.

Gallagher, Buell G. *American Caste and the Negro College.* New York: Columbia University Press, 1938.

Gustafson, James M. *Treasure in Earthen Vessels: The Church as a Human Community.* New York: Harper and Bros., 1961.

Haselden, Kyle. *The Racial Problem in Christian Perspective.* New York: Harper and Bros., 1959.

Holmes, Dwight O.W. *The Evolution of the Negro College.* New York: Teachers College, Columbia University, 1934.

Horton, Douglas. *Congregationalism: A Study in Church Polity.* London: Independent Press, 1952.

Hotchkiss, Wesley A. *A Door So Wide.* Centennial Series. New York: American Missionary Association, 1965.

International Congregational Council—Committee of One Hundred. *The Gospel, the Church and Society: Congregationalism Today.* New York: General Council of Congregational Christian Churches, 1938.

Jenkins, Daniel. *Congregationalism: A Restatement.* London: Faber and Faber, 1959.

Johnson, Charles S. et al. *To Stem This Tide: A Survey of Racial Tension Areas in the United States.* Boston: Pilgrim Press, 1943.

Johnson, Charles S., Embree, Edwin R., and Alexander, W.W. *The Collapse of Cotton Tenancy.* Chapel Hill, N.C.: University of North Carolina Press, 1935.

Lenski, Gerhard. *The Religious Factor: A Sociological Study of Religion's Impact on Politics, Economics, and Family Life.* Garden City, N.Y.: Doubleday, 1961.

Loescher, Frank S. *The Protestant Church and the Negro.* New York: Association Press, 1948.

Logan, Rayford W. *The Negro in the United States.* Princeton: D. Van Nostrand Co., 1957.

McIntyre, John. *The Christian Doctrine of History.* Edinburgh: Oliver and Boyd, 1957.

Mays, Benjamin E., and Nicholson, Joseph William. *The Negro's Church.* New York: Institute of Social and Religious Research, 1933.

Merton, Robert K. *Social Theory and Social Structure*. Chicago: Free Press, 1957.

Métraux, Alfred. *Voodoo in Haiti*. Translated by Hugo Charteris. New York: Schocken Books, 1972.

Myrdal, Gunnar. *An American Dilemma: The Negro Problem and Modern Democracy*. New York: Harper and Bros., 1944.

Niebuhr, H. Richard. *The Kingdom of God in America*. Chicago: Willet, Clark & Co., 1937.

————. *The Social Sources of Denominationalism*. New York: Henry Holt and Co., 1929.

Olmstead, Clifton E. *History of Religion in the United States*. Englewood Cliffs, N.J.: Prentice-Hall, 1960.

Pipes, William H. *Say Amen, Brother! Old-Time Negro Preaching: A Study in American Frustration*. New York: William-Frederick Press, 1951.

Pope, Liston. *The Kingdom Beyond Caste*. New York: Friendship Press, 1957.

Radin, Paul, ed. *God Struck Me Dead: Religious Conversion Experiences and Autobiographies of Negro Ex-Slaves*. Nashville: Social Science Institute, Fisk University, 1945.

Ramsey, Paul, ed. *Faith and Ethics: The Theology of H. Richard Niebuhr*. New York: Harper and Bros., 1957.

Richardson, Alan. *A Theological Word Book of the Bible*. New York: Macmillan, 1950.

Richardson, Harry V. *Dark Glory: A Picture of the Church Among Negroes in the Rural South*. New York: Friendship Press, 1947.

Simpson, G.E., and Yinger, J.M. *Racial and Cultural Minorities*. New York: Harper and Bros., 1953.

Stein, Joseph H. *Pilgrimage Toward Unity*. Boston: Pilgrim Press, 1957.

Survey, vol. 70, January 1916.

Thurman, Howard. *Jesus and the Disinherited*. New York: Abingdon-Cokesbury Press, 1949.

Troeltsch, Ernst. *The Social Teaching of the Christian Churches*. Translated by Olive Wyon. New York: Macmillan, 1931.

Weaver, Robert C. *Negro Labor: A National Problem*. New York: Harcourt, Brace and Co., 1946.

Welch, Claude. *The Reality of the Church*. New York: Charles Scribner's Sons, 1958.

Wilmore, Gayraud. *Black Religion and Black Radicalism*. Garden City, N.Y.: Doubleday, 1973.

Wilson, James Q. *Negro Politics: The Search for Leadership*. Chicago: Free Press, 1960.

Woodson, Carter G. *The History of the Negro Church*. 2d ed. Washington, D.C.: Associated Publishers, 1921.

————. *The Rural Negro.*Washington: The Association for the Study of Negro Life and History, 1930.

Work, Monroe N. *Negro Year Book*. Tuskegee Institute, Ala.: Negro Year Book Co.

Index of Names and Places

Abolitionists, 23
  New England Reunion of
    (June 1864), 23
Adams, John Q., 20
African Methodist Episcopal
    Church Zion, ix
Alabama, 76, 92
  Athens, 44
  Birmingham, 85, 91
  Florence, 44
  Marion, 44
  Montgomery, 44, 78, 85
  Selma, 55, 68
  Talladega, 44, 55, 67
Alexander, W.S., 123, 126, 129
Allen Normal, 44
American Board of
    Commissioners for
    Foreign Missions, 22
American Missionary
    (magazine), 23, 81, 121-33,
    141-51
  1859, 39
  1863, 60
  1866, 46, 53
  1869, 29
  1874, 49
  1877, 40
  1913, 81
American Missionary
    Association, ix, passim
  Alabama Association, 69

Annual Meeting of 1882
    (Cleveland), 70
  1912 (Buffalo), 89
  1913 (Kansas City), 89
Annual Report of 1911-1912
    (Sixty-sixth), 73
  1913 (Sixty-seventh),
    89-90
Central South Conference,
  68
Committee on Church Work,
  70
Constitution; Article Three,
  89
First national meeting of
    (1848-Hartford), 23
Foreign Fields, 20-21
Home Mission Department,
  20
Incorporated, 49
Mendi Mission, 20, 59
American Protestant Church,
  32
Amistad, 20
Amistad Committee, 20, 23
Arkansas
  Helena, 41, 44
  Little Rock, 42, 85
Armistead, Helen, xii
Ashley, S.S., 121
Atlanta University, 44, 68
Avery Institute, 44, 75

Ballard Normal, 44
Ballou, Hosea, 50
Baptists, 33, 36
Barnwell, Henry S., 93-94
Barth, Karl, 8
Beach Institute, 44
Beard, Augustus Field, 19, 46, 59, 75
Beecher, Henry Ward, 23
Berea College, 44
Bennett, Lerone, 103
Black Bourgeoisie (Frazier), 74-75
Blade, Jack, 97-98
Bothwell, Pastor, 130
Bradford, William, 13
Brick Junior College, 43
  Franklinton Center, 43
  Rural Life School, 43
Brown, Henry E., 67
Brownlee, Fred L., 93-94
Bull, Edward, 64-65
Burrell Normal, 44
Butler, General, 21

Canal Street Presbyterian Church, 128
Census of 1790, 30
Congregational Church (at Charleston), 50
Central Congregational Church (New Orleans), 121-23, 125-26, 128-33
Chandler Normal, 44
Charleston Daily News, 75
Chase, Mrs. T.N., 125
Christian Endeavor Orchestra, 132
  Society, 132
Church of England, 11-13
Colored Sanitary Association, 132

Committee for West Indian Missions, 20
Congregational Associations and Conferences, 24, 68
Congregational Church, ix, passim
  Board of Home Missions, 151-52
  Board of Ministerial Relief, 151
  Christian Church, ix
  Church Building Society, 89, 133, 151
  Education Society, 151
  National Council of Congregational Churches, 24-25, 54, 70, 84, 88-89, 142
  Publishing Society (Pilgrim Press), 151
  Sunday School Extension Society, 151
Congregationalism: A Study in Church Polity (Horton), 7, 14
Congregationalist, The, 54-55
Connecticut, 49
  Hartford, 23, 49
  New Haven, 49
  Torrington, 50
  West Hartford, 50
Convention of the South, ix
Cripps, Mrs. M.F., 132
Crusade of Brotherhood, A (Beard), 19

DeMond, Abraham Lincoln, 131
Dillard University, 45, 68
Dixwell Avenue Congregational Church (New Haven), 49

168

Tade, E.D., 147-48
Taft, William Howard, 84
Talcott Street Church, 49
Talladega College, 44-45, 67, 93, 144-47
  Seminary, 69, 93, 145-47
Tennessee
  Chattanooga, 55, 85, 147-49
  Memphis, 41, 44, 55, 78, 85
  Nashville, 42, 44, 55, 82, 85
Texas
  Austin, 44
  Dallas, 85
  Houston, ix
Thompson, C.H., 121
Tillotson, 44-45
Tougaloo University, 44-45, 67
Treasure in Earthen Vessels: The Church as a Human Community (Gustafson) 87-88
Trinity School, 44
Troeltsch, Ernst, 3-5

Union Missionary Society, 20
United Church of Christ
  Conferences, ix
U.S. Marine Hospital Service, 132

Virginia, 22
  Appomattox, 23
  Arlington Heights, 42
  Capahosic, 43
  Croney Island, 41
  Ferry Point, 42

Fortress Monroe, 21-22, 41, 149
  Hampton, 41, 43, 150
  Jamestown, 30
  Newport News (Camp Butler), 21, 141
  Norfolk, 41-42
  Portsmouth, 41
  Yorktown, 41
Voodoo in Haiti (Métraux), 34

Walker, Thompson, 151
Washburn Seminary, 44
Washington, Booker T., 131
Washington, D.C., 41, 43, 78
Welch, Claude, 10
Wesleyan Methodists, 22
West Virginia
  Harpers Ferry, 42
Western Evangelical
  Missionary Society for
  Work Among the
  American Indians, 20
Wharton, James, 66, 127-28, 130
White, Hugh Vernon, 15
Woodson, Carter, ix
Wool, General, 22
Wright, Leon, xii
Wyckoff, A.N., 128

Young Men's Christian
  Association, 130
  of the City of New York, 21-22, 141

172